# REAL LIFE IN CHRIST

# REAL LIFE IN CHRIST

*T. B. Maston*

BROADMAN PRESS

Nashville, Tennessee

© Copyright 1974 • Broadman Press
Nashville, Tennessee
All rights reserved
4219–23
ISBN: 0–8054–1923–3
Dewey Decimal Classification: 248.8
Library of Congress Catalog Card Number: 73–87066
Printed in the United States of America

To
Missionary Friends
with whom these
messages
have been shared

# PREFACE

This project has evolved from several deepening convictions. One is that an outstanding, if not *the* outstanding, weakness of contemporary Christianity is the poor quality of Christian living by many who claim to be followers of Christ. This weakness stems from certain other weaknesses. One of these is a failure to understand the basic nature of the Christian life. It has been considered too largely in terms of certain formalities such as making a profession of faith, being voted into the fellowship of a church, being baptized, attending faithfully the services of the church, and giving tithes and offerings to help support the church's program. These are expressions of the Christian life, but they do not touch the vitalities or depths of that life. Furthermore, they are largely meaningless unless they have been preceded and are accompanied by a vital Christian experience.

Another deepening conviction has been that a considerable number of the members of churches of different denominations are increasingly aware of the basic weakness of contemporary Christianity, and as a result they are searching for new depths in their Christian faith. They feel that there is something deeper and more significant than they have so far discovered. Also, they believe that they must go deeper before their activity for Christ and his church can be most meaningful to them, to others, and to the cause of Christ. This book was written primarily for these searching souls, some of whom are in the pulpit, others in the pew, some of whom are adults while others are Christian youth.

Most of this material has been used with groups of students, laymen, pastors, and particularly with foreign missionaries. The response has been favorable, several suggesting that it should be published. There are two ways in which these studies differ from most devotional books. First, they are largely exegetical studies of particular passages of Scripture. Second, the major attempt is to challenge rather than to comfort.

Although considerable study has gone into the preparation of the messages, it has been considered wise to eliminate footnotes. References are made in the body of the material by the use of abbreviations to various translations [see list following preface] and to commentaries that follow a verse-by-verse format [see list of resources in back of book]. It is believed that this will make for easier reading. These studies will be more helpful to you if you will have an open Bible readily available. The use of several versions for comparison will also be helpful.

Although there are references to many versions of the Bible, the Revised Standard Version was used except when otherwise indicated.

Appreciation is expressed to those who have encouraged publication of the studies and to Mrs. Melvin Bridgford, who has prepared the manuscript for publication.

T. B. Maston

# TRANSLATIONS

# CONTENTS

# CONTENTS

# CHAPTER I

# The New Life

*Therefore, if any one is in Christ, he is a new creation; the old has passed away, behold, the new has come.*—2 Corinthians 5:17

It was my junior year at Central High School, Fountain City, Tennessee. We had been on a football trip to Asheville, North Carolina. One of our players was injured. We had to leave him behind in a hospital. The Lord used that experience to convict me of my need for Christ.

There was a revival meeting the next week in the church where some of my family belonged and where I had been attending Sunday School. During that week and particularly as I walked home after dark from football practice, a battle was being fought within my mind and soul. Each night Dad or "Sis" would ask me to go to the revival with them. I gave the excuse that I had to study. Friday night I could not give that excuse. Also, we did not have a football game the next day.

That Friday night, November 13, in Smithwood Baptist Church, then a small country church but now a thriving suburban church, something happened to me that changed the whole direction of my life. My response to the inner prompting of the divine Spirit and the invitation of the pastor came as the congregation was singing that grand old gospel song:

> Just as I am,
>   without one plea,
> But that thy blood
>   was shed for me,
> And that Thou bidd'st
>   me come to Thee,
> O Lamb of God,
>   I come! I come!

On Sunday, two days after that experience, as I was walking through the pasture field on the way to Sunday School and church, the thought came to me, *These two days with Jesus have been worth more than all the rest of my life put together.*

Your experience was not the same as mine. You may not even remember the time and place but you do know that some time in the past you "met the Master face to face" and entered into life in him. How can you and I explain what happened to us?

A major source of help is a study of the Scriptures. One of the most helpful passages regarding the nature of the initial experience is Paul's statement in 2 Corinthians 5:17 with the verses immediately preceding and following it. (It is hoped that you have an open Bible before you as we begin these studies together. It will be helpful if you have several translations readily available.)

### Its Nature

Notice that Paul did not say if any man is "of Christ"

or "of the Christ party" but "if any one is *in Christ,* he is a new creation," "a new being" (TEV), "a new person altogether" (Phillips), or "a brand new person inside" (TLB). The new creation is a result of being in Christ. One commentator says that the picture is of a sphere or circle; Christ fills the sphere or circle as Savior and Lord. If we are "in Christ" we are in the circle with him. Within this sphere or circle there is communion with Christ, and such communion or fellowship in and with Christ is the essence of being a Christian.

Whether or not we fully understand it at the time of our initial experience with the Lord, we were brought into a vital, life-changing union with the resurrected Christ. We are in him and he is in us. It is in him that we have been made alive (Rom. 8:10). Our union with him is our hope of glory (Col. 1:27).

As you know, the two words "in Christ" are very prominent in Paul's epistles. They are *a* key, if not *the* key expression of his thought. Deissmann says that this and comparable expressions occur one hundred and sixty-four times in Paul's letters, and that "in Christ" is "the characteristic expression" of his religious thought (p. 171). The renowned Scottish preacher and teacher, James Stewart, in *Man in Christ,* similarly says that "the heart of Paul's religion is union with Christ" (p. 147), that "in Christ" is "the most characteristic phrase in the apostle's terminology" (p. 155). The English New Testament scholar, William Barclay, suggests that "in Christ" is "the centre and soul" of Paul's Christian experience and the summary of his religion (*Mind of St. Paul,* p. 121). Paul himself said, "I have been crucified with Christ; it is no longer

I who live, but Christ who lives in me" (Gal. 2:20). The following are only a few of the many references of Paul to his use of "in Christ":

Romans 8:1—"There is therefore now no condemnation for those who are in Christ Jesus"

Romans 12:5—"So we, though many, are one body in Christ"

1 Corinthians 3:1—"babes in Christ"

1 Corinthians 4:10—"wise in Christ"

1 Corinthians 15:18—"fallen asleep in Christ"

1 Corinthians 15:22—"in Christ shall all be made alive"

2 Corinthians 1:21—"God . . . establishes us with you in Christ"

2 Corinthians 2:14—"God . . . in Christ leads us in triumph"

Galatians 2:4—"freedom . . . in Christ Jesus"

Ephesians 1:3—"blessed us in Christ"

Ephesians 3:6—"partakers of the promise in Christ Jesus"

Philippians 2:1—"encouragement in Christ"

Philippians 3:14—"the upward call of God in Christ Jesus"

In most places where Paul used "in Christ," "in Christ Jesus," or similar terms he refers to the mystical union of the believer with the risen Lord.

The relationship of the believer to Christ is so vital that Jesus compared it to the relation of the vine and the branches. He said, "I am the vine, you are the branches" (John 15:5). The branches are not something apart from the vine. They are an integral part of the vine. The lifeblood of the vine flows through the branches. Their fruitfulness is a result and an evidence of their vital relationship to the vine.

This new creation, which results from one's union with Christ, is a possibility for all men. Notice it says "if any one is in Christ." How grateful we should be for the blessed "whosoevers" of the gospel, for the universal invitation for men to come to Christ as Savior and Lord! If this were not true, some of us might have been left out. All of the deep and abundant riches that are available to any man in Christ are equally available to all men who will come to him.

## Its Results

What are some of the results of the new life we have through union with Christ? Paul suggests that "the old has passed away"—a decisive past act: "the past is finished and gone" (Phillips). We may still be hampered by the carnal, fleshly nature, but we are now "in Christ." The "in Christ" makes a difference. There is a sense in which the old has passed away but its influence lingers on. The ultimate victory over the old way of life, however, is so certain that that which is only a potentiality now can be seen and spoken of as a present reality.

The vacuum left by the passing of the old is filled with the new. In a vividly dramatic, triumphant note Paul said, "Behold, all things are become new" (KJV). This is true even if the "old man" still clings to us "like bits of eggshell to the young chick." At least we are out of the shell. The prospects of the new are before us.

What passed away and what was and is new in the

new life we have in Christ? For at least a partial answer let us look back at verses 14–16. Paul said, "No longer, then, do we judge anyone by human standards" (TEV) or "by the standard of outward appearances" (v. 16, Williams). Paul had a different perspective concerning his fellowman. For Paul the old distinctions based on culture, class, or color had passed away. These things "cut no figure now with Paul (Gal. 3:28) as he looks at men from the standpoint of the cross of Christ" (Robertson). This change in perspective stemmed from Paul's understanding that Christ had died for all and all had been united with him in his death: his death was in a real sense their death (v. 14). The death of Christ and the death of the believer in Christ means, among other things, that all carnal or fleshly distinctions also died. The one important thing for one who is in Christ is the relation of his fellowmen to Christ.

Paul no longer even thought of Christ as he had formerly. He did not judge him after the flesh—the earthly Jesus. For Paul and other early Christians the supreme thing was Christ as a present power rather than Jesus as a historic person. Their faith was centered in the Christ who had died and through the resurrection had been "let loose in the world."

Also, Paul revealed that old ambitions, motives, purposes, and values were replaced with new ones. Because Christ died for us, we should no longer live for ourselves but for him who for our sakes died and was raised (v. 15). We regret that we have to say that this is what *should* be true in our lives. In this as well as many other areas there is "a gaping chasm between words and deeds."

When we contemplate the marvelous blessings,

potential and real, that are ours through our union with Christ, should we not and can we not join Paul in saying, "The love of Christ controls" us (v. 14) "continuously constrains" us (Williams), or has us in its "inescapable grasp" (Moffatt)? This love presses us on every side, holding us to our task whatever others may think or say. This love that controls, constrains, or presses us is not our love for Christ but his love for us (see Rom. 5:5; 8:35, 39; 15:30; Eph. 2:4; 2 Thess. 3:5). Our understanding of the love of Christ for us can and should become the greatest possible dynamic in our lives.

Let us return for a moment to the last words of verse 17, "Behold, the new has come." The new life we have in Christ looks back to the old ways that have been put away, but it also looks forward to the new that has come and yet is continuously coming. *The New English Bible* says, "A new order has already begun." Similarly, *The Living Bible* says, "A new life has begun!" It has begun but it is not complete and will not be until we awake in his likeness. We are "in Christ" the moment we in faith open our lives to him, but we must grow up into him in all things. The full attainment of the new is a continuing process. The process, however, is based and dependent upon a very real and abiding change in the direction of our lives.

Our union with Christ not only brings into our lives new ambitions, motives, purposes, and perspectives; how glorious it is also to remember that it brings us into contact with a new source of power. Without him we can do nothing (John 15:5), but we can join Paul in saying, "I can do all things in him who strengthens me" (Phil. 4:13). How completely the latter is true in our lives depends on how fully we abide in him and let him abide in us. The power to live victoriously for Christ rests in him. James Stewart, in his particularly graphic, dynamic way, says that "Christ in me" is something more than an impossible ideal or a pattern beyond our imitation. He says, " 'Christ in me' means Christ bearing me along from within, Christ the motive-power that carries me on, Christ giving my whole life a wonderful poise and lift, and turning every burden into wings" (p. 169).

### Its Source

Paul plainly revealed in verses 18 and 19 the source of the experience that makes us new creations in Christ and the source of the results that flow from that experience: "All this is from God," "This all originated with God" (Williams), "From first to last this has been the work of God" (NEB). Through our union with Christ we become new creations and this new creation has the same source or author as the first creation. God is not only the Creator but also the Re-Creator.

Paul further said that "God . . . through Christ reconciled us to himself," "changed us from enemies into his friends" (TEV). The "us" here evidently referred to Paul, but in the next verse he said that "God was in Christ reconciling the world to himself" (v. 19). God was the source of the reconciliation of Paul but he is also the source of reconciliation for you and me. The reconciliation is achieved "through Christ" (v. 18) or "in Christ" (v. 19). God is the prime mover in the reconciliation; Christ is the agent or instrument of the reconciliation (cf. Rom. 5:11). We may not understand all that is involved in the reconciliation, but there is no doubt that it originates with God.

Another way of saying much the same thing is to say that we have been saved by grace through faith; and that this salvation is not our own doing but the gift of God—not of works lest we should boast. "For we are his workmanship, created in Christ Jesus for good works" (Eph. 2:8–10). Good works may be and is the purpose of salvation but there is no doubt about the source of salvation. We are his workmanship or craftmanship; then notice the striking similarity to 2 Corinthians 5:17: "created in Christ Jesus." The creation takes place through our union with him. Our part is to accept in faith the grace of God as revealed and offered to us in Christ.

### Its Purpose

There is abundant evidence in the Scriptures that there is always a purpose in the initial Christian experience that goes far beyond the experience itself. When we say that we are saved, we usually mean saved from the final penalty of sin (from hell) and saved for an abiding fellowship with our Lord (for heaven). These are glorious truths but there is something else involved in our experience with the Lord. As Paul said in Ephesians 2:10, we are created in Christ Jesus *for,* for the purpose of, or with a view to good works, good deeds, or a life of goodness.

The passage in 2 Corinthians that we have used as the main basis for our study suggests two or three purposes of the experience that makes us children of God. For example, as a result of our own reconciliation he "gave us the ministry of reconciliation" (v. 18b), "entrusting to us the message of reconciliation" (v. 19b). Our minds and hearts are the depository of that message, which we are to share with the world. Our chief business as children of God is to be channels for the reconciling love of God. This reconciling love of God not only reconciles man to God but as an inevitable by-product it also reconciles man to his fellow-man. Sin separates. The love of God in our hearts unites the estranged.

We as well as Paul are "ambassadors for Christ" (v. 20a; cf. Eph. 6:20) or on the behalf of Christ. The ambassador speaks and acts, not for himself, but for the ruler or country he represents. He is his ruler's mouthpiece or his country's representative. In a sense, he is not responsible for the content of the message he delivers; he is responsible for the accurate transmission of that message. God makes his appeal through his ambassadors. It is quite important to remember that "the ambassador has to be *persona grata* with both countries (the one he represents and the one to which he goes)" (Robertson).

The purpose of the appeal we make as ambassadors of Christ is that men might be reconciled to God. The heart of the appeal for reconciliation is the fact that Christ who knew no sin was made sin "for us" (v. 21, KJV). The words "who knew no sin" evidently refer to the fact that Jesus was not conscious of sin in his life. He himself asked the question, which, incidentally, has never been answered: "Which of you convicts me of sin?" (John 8:46). Peter testified that "he committed no sin" (1 Pet. 2:22), while John said that "in him there is no sin" (1 John 3:5). The writer of Hebrews said that our high priest is "one who in every respect has been tempted as we are, yet without sinning" (Heb. 4:15). It is this One who knew no sin and who died for us with whom we have been brought into union.

Notice in the latter part of verse 21 another purpose of our union with Christ: "So that [a statement of purpose] in him we might become the righteousness of God," "might come into right standing with God" (Williams). Through our union with Christ we have been reconciled to God, which means, among other things, that we have been made righteous in his sight or brought into right standing with him. Because we are in Christ we are treated as righteous by God. It is also true that through our union with him some of the righteousness or goodness of God becomes ours. There always lingers, however, enough of the old sinful nature that to be treated as righteous by God is the work of his grace. Let us heed the admonition of Paul, "We entreat you not to accept the grace of God in vain" (2 Cor. 6:1).

There are certainly other purposes that evolve from the new life we have in Christ. The main thing is for us to recognize that the experience that made us new creations was purposeful and in a sense preparatory. You remember that Paul, when he met the resurrected Christ on the Damascus road, was told to go into the city and it would be told him what he was to do (Acts 9:6). There was something for him to do about the experience he had had. God had a purpose for the life of Paul; the experience on the way to Damascus was the initial step in the fulfillment of that purpose. It was to Ananias that the Lord revealed that Paul was a chosen instrument to carry his message to "the Gentiles and kings and the sons of Israel" (Acts 9:15). Paul's life was an expanding experience with and within the will and purpose of God, a purpose that was in the plan of God even before Paul was blinded on the Damascus road. The latter was used by the Lord to start Paul in the right direction, in the direction of his will for his life.

What about your experience and mine? Could it be when we were brought into union with Christ that God was using that experience to begin his revelation to us of his will and purpose for our lives? Was that experience the initial and necessary step in an expanding consciousness of his purpose? Could it be that when God saved me as a sixteen-year-old he had in mind that I would give most of my life to teaching in a theological seminary? I personally believe he did, although some of my students through the years doubtlessly have had some questions about my being within the will of God.

We can be sure of this: There is a divine purpose at work in our initial experience and in every subsequent experience we have with the Lord. One purpose that is common to all of us as children of God is that we might live a life that would honor the One who lives within us.

Now, how can we sum up what we have attempted to say? What does it mean to be a Christian? It means to be brought into a vital, life-changing union with the resurrected Christ.

What does it mean to be a *real* Christian? We can sum it up by saying that it means to let that which was a potentiality in the initial experience become a living, dynamic reality in our lives. In other words, it means to let the resurrected Christ live in us and express himself through us.

What would it mean if we let him live in us and express himself through us? A study of the kind of life he lived while he walked among men would be helpful to us. We would find, among other things, that he was interested in all kinds of people, that he had compassion on people, and that "he went about doing good" (Acts 10:38). Here is enough to challenge us to the end of life's journey.

Thank God: We are in Christ and he is in us! May we so let him live in us that he will increasingly be revealed to others through us!

# CHAPTER II

# The Transformed Life

*Do not be conformed to this world but be transformed by the renewal of your mind, that you may prove what is the will of God, what is good and acceptable and perfect.*—Romans 12:2

It was suggested in our previous discussion that when we were brought into union with Christ we became new creations or new persons altogether. Since this is true, do we need the admonition of Paul, "Do not be conformed . . . but be transformed"? Will we not agree that although we have become new creations in Christ Jesus, yet in a very real sense the creation is incomplete? It is process as well as achievement. To use the terminology of the present discussion, we have been transformed but we are also in the process of being transformed. This process will continue for the remainder of our lives. This means that Paul's admonition is applicable to us today.

## Background for the Exhortation

As you know, some of Paul's epistles, such as Romans, are primarily theological. Even in these epistles he came in the latter part of them to some practical applications. These applications or exhortations were based upon or derived from what he had previously said. The transition from the more theoretical and theological portion of the epistle to the more practical or ethical was frequently made by the use of a "therefore" (Rom. 12:1; Eph. 4:1).

"Therefore" is a very important word in the Bible as a whole but particularly in Paul's epistles. It was his "stop, look, listen" word. He was about to say something important which was directly related to something he had previously said. The "therefore" of Romans 12:1 provides an introduction to all the exhortations in chapters 12 to 15. If this were kept in mind, it would give added weight or impact to each exhortation. The latter is particularly true of Romans 12:2. It might be read as follows: "I beseech you therefore, brethren, by the mercies of God do not be conformed to this world. . . ."

What were the "mercies of God" that provided the background or basis for Paul's exhortations? My judgment is that the reference was to all that he had said in the first eleven chapters of Romans. In broad outline Paul had said: (1) that all men have sinned, (2) that all are under condemnation for sin, (3) that the way of salvation through or by faith is available to all men, and (4) that this salvation brings some marvelous blessings. Among these are: freedom from the enslavement of sin, freedom from the condemnation of the law, and the opportunity of being in the family of God with all its wonderful privileges.

These and numerous other mercies or blessings of God continue to place all of us under obligation to him. The ethical demands of our faith are based upon the grace of God, which is the source of all his mercies. The "therefore" in our lives binds together what we believe and what we do and are. There is a unity of doctrine and the daily life.

## The Exhortation

Moses commanded, Paul implored or exhorted. His appeal was to gratitude rather than to fear. The hope for a favorable response to such an appeal or exhortation is the fact that the child of God has been brought into union with the resurrected Christ. Although we cannot escape entirely the drag or resistance of our sinful human nature, there is something within us that prods us to respond favorably to the exhortation to live a transformed life. The more fully we are acquainted with the mercies of God, the more readily we will respond favorably to the challenge to walk in the ways of the Lord.

Notice that the exhortation in Romans 12:2 is both *negative* and *positive*. This twofold emphasis is typical of Paul and of the Bible as a whole. For example, in the Old Testament the children of Israel were called to be a holy people; separated from the world and the peoples of the world but also separated unto God and his purposes (see Lev. 20:26). As Christians we have been *saved from* some things but also *saved to* or *for* some things. We are to *put off* the old man or nature and *put on* "the new nature, created after the likeness of God in true righteousness and holiness" (Eph. 4:24).

Paul's *negative exhortation* was: "Do not be conformed to this world" or "Don't copy the behaviour and witness of this world" (TLB). Phillips' particularly graphic translation is, "Don't let the world around you squeeze you into its own mould."

There are two words in the New Testament translated "world": *aion* and *kosmos*. The former, the word used in Romans 12:2, in its various forms is translated "world," "age," or "ever" or a combination of "ever": forever, ever and ever, everlasting. About two thirds of the time *aion* receives the last translation. The other word, *kosmos*, is used considerably more frequently than *aion*, over four times as often for "age" or "world." *Kosmos* is a rather distinctive Johannine word, being found in John's writings almost as many times as in all the remainder of the New Testament. Of the two translations of *aion*, "age" or "world," the King James Version practically always translates it "world," while the Revised Standard Version most frequently translates it "age" (e.g., Matt. 28:20), Romans 12:2 being an example. *Aion* is used at times with a negative or critical connotation: "the god of this world" (2 Cor. 4:4), "this present evil age" ("world," KJV, Gal. 1:4). *Kosmos* at times is inclusive of the peoples of the world: "God so loved the world" (John 3:16), "I am the light of the world" (John 8:12).

The world or age that Paul referred to here (Rom. 12:2) is temporal or transient in contrast to the age to come which is permanent or eternal. We who have the eternal dwelling within us and who are looking for a Kingdom that is eternal should not let the world that passes away squeeze us into its mold. This exhortation may apply to some degree to dress and style of life but far more important are the motives, purposes, and values of the contemporary world or age.

The verb "conform" carries the idea of continuous action: "Stop being fashioned" or "do not have the habit" of being conformed to the world (Robertson). This implies that conformity to the world is a process. It usually comes about by imperceptible stages. One step may and usually will lead to another. Lot, the nephew of Abraham, is a good illustration of the progressive nature of conformity to the world. When Abraham gave Lot the opportunity to choose, he "lifted up his eyes, and saw the Jordan valley was well watered" (Gen. 13:10). He chose the Jordan valley, he "moved his tent as far as Sodom" (Gen. 13:12), he "dwelt in Sodom" (Gen. 14:12), he sat "in the gate of Sodom" (Gen. 19:1)—he had become a leader in the city. Have you ever observed a friend or a member of your church who started to drift away from the Lord and his church? On most occasions it was just "one little step" at a time until he was almost completely absorbed in the world and the things of the world. What is more pointed, have you had that experience yourself?

The second or *positive* part of the exhortation is as follows: "but let God transform you inwardly" (TEV). Williams, as usual, brings out the verb tense: "continue to transform yourself." The transformation is a process just as is true of conformity to the world. But is Williams correct in suggesting that we can transform ourselves? The transformation cannot take place without our cooperation but transformation is a work of grace just as much as the initial experience when we became children of God. Paul, writing to the Corinthians, said, "And we all . . . are being changed into his likeness from one degree of glory to another; for this comes from the Lord who is the Spirit" (2 Cor. 3:18). Notice: (1) we "are being changed into his likeness from one degree of glory to another." We have been changed but we are also being changed. (2) The process as well as the original experience is the work of the Lord: "This comes from the Lord who is the Spirit." The word translated "changed" is another form of the same word translated "transformed" in Romans 12:2.

The root of the "word is *morphe,* and *morphe* means the essential unchanging shape or element of anything." The change or transformation Paul is talking about is not a change of outer form but "of the very essence of our being" (Barclay). It is an inner change, a transformation of the essential man. To use an English word derived from the Greek—a metamorphosis has taken place when there is "a marked or complete change of character."

Will you not agree that the exhortation by Paul, "Do not be conformed to this world but be transformed," is needed by all of us as individual Christians and by our churches? They and we who compose them are pressed by a world that seeks to squeeze them and us into its mold.

### Means for the Transformation

The transformation is "by the renewal of your mind." "Let your minds be remade and your whole nature thus transformed" (NEB).

As used in the Bible, "mind" is more than intellect. There are places where it seems to be closely related to if not actually identified or equated with will or purpose. For example, Paul said, "But we have the mind of Christ'' (1 Cor. 2:16). He evidently meant purpose or intent of Christ. We use ''mind'' in a similar way.

What is meant by ''the renewal of your mind''? It may help us to know that there are two words for new. One of these, *neos*, means ''new in point of time.'' The other, *kainos*, means ''new in point of character and nature.'' Sometimes the following distinction is made: *neos* = young in contrast to old; *kainos* = fresh in contrast to worn or stale. It is the latter word (*kainos*) that is used here—renewed or refreshed in character and nature. Such renewal is the work of the divine Spirit.

Does renewal in Romans 12:2 refer to *the initial experience* when one comes into union with the living Christ? Or, was Paul referring to *a continuing experience* or to a *progressive renewal*? We have been renewed but we are also in the process of being renewed. The renewal is never complete. It must take place again and again. It seems to me that Paul's reference here was to this progressive concept. The choice of the word implies this. Our inner life, our character, our relations with the Lord are in constant need of renewal or refreshing. Furthermore, Paul was writing to a Christian group. His appeal in 12:1 was that they present their bodies a living sacrifice. Now his appeal is that their minds, their inner natures, be renewed and thus their lives would be transformed. This makes the entire exhortation immediately relevant to you and to me, to all of us who claim to be children of God.

There are some illustrations in the Scriptures that suggest that outer transformation results from inner change. When Moses came down from the mount, you remember that he "did not know that the skin of his face shone." What was the source of the shining face of Moses? The Scripture plainly says, "because he had been talking with God" (Ex. 34:29). Spending those days on the mount in communication with God, some of the glory that belonged to God had become a part of Moses. It was inner with an outer manifestation. But incidentally, notice that Moses was unconscious of the fact that his face shone. Those saints of God who reveal something of God's glory because of their close association with him are seldom if ever conscious of that fact.

You also remember the incident of the transfiguration of Jesus. Matthew says that he "was transfigured before them: and his face shone like the sun, and his garments became white as light" (Matt. 17:2; cf. Mark 9:2). Did you know that the word translated "transfigured" here is the same word as the one translated "transformed" in Romans 12:2? The latter could be translated, "be transfigured." What was the secret to or the source of the transfiguration of Jesus? Luke reveals the secret. He says, "And as he was praying, the appearance of his countenance was altered, and his raiment became dazzling white" (Luke 9:29). As he was praying his communication and fellowship with the Father became so close and intimate that something of the glory that he had had with the Father before he came into the world became his again. His inner, divine nature was revealed.

## Purpose of the Transformation

There are two clearly stated but closely related purposes or results of being transformed or transfigured.

One is that we may prove, *know* (KJV), discern (NEB), or know surely (Interpreter's) *what the will of God is*. "An unrenewed mind cannot know the will of God" (Expositors'). A transformed life, the product of an inner renewal, has a deepened sensitivity to the leadership of the Holy Spirit.

The maturing child of God is on a constant search for the will of God. He wants to know that will, not primarily that he may meditate upon it, but that he may be obedient to it. He recognizes that the supreme authority for him is the will of God. It is not what he thinks but what God thinks; not what his group, his gang, his family, or even his church approves, but what God approves. This means that it is tremendously important for us to know the will of God.

It is only the transformed life, which results from an inner renewal, that can know or discern the will of God. Even then, that knowledge or discernment will never be perfect or complete. The deeper the inner renewal the more clearly we will see the breadth and the depth of the will of God. We will increasingly discern that God has a will for every area of our lives and every area of the life of the world. A constant renewal or refreshing of our inner life in the Lord is needed if we are to respond and be obedient to that will. One phase of the renewal must be a willingness and even a desire to do the will of God once it is known. It is the seeking mind and the willing heart that will know his will.

Living the transformed life will not only enable us to know the will of God, it will also help us to understand the nature of that will: that it is good, acceptable, and perfect. The three words—"good," "acceptable," and "perfect"—either define the will of God or describe its content. Which is meant makes little if any difference. The main thing for us to remember is that it is only the renewed mind that can comprehend or understand that the will of God is good, acceptable, and perfect. And the more fully or completely the inner life is renewed the clearer will be our understanding of the nature of the will of God. As we consider the three elements or characteristics of the will of God, let us reverse the order for some brief comments.

Paul suggested that the will of God was perfect, whole, or complete. It is all-inclusive. His will is as broad as life. It could not be otherwise since he is the sovereign God of the universe. His will is all-inclusive for your life and mine.

But since God's will is perfect or whole it also includes every aspect of the life of the home, the church, the community, the nation, the world. For example, God has a will for the relation of men and women, of employers and employees, of different classes and races, and of various nations and civilizations.

His will is not only all-inclusive; it also demands or expects full maturity or perfection. It is held out before us constantly to challenge us while at the same time we realize that we can never fully attain it or give expression to it. The deeper the renewal, the more complete the transformation, the more clearly we will see that the will of God is perfect and beyond our grasp. It sounds paradoxical but the more we live the transformed life the more we will realize that we do not understand fully the will of God. There is progress in knowing as well as doing his will.

The preceding will never be used by the renewed mind, the transformed life to justify a low level of living. Rather, the one who has been transformed or possibly better, who is being transformed, will feel a constant tug to move up higher, to know more fully, and to be more obedient to the will of God.

The more mature we become the more "acceptable" will be the will of God not only to God but to us. One reason for its acceptability is the fact that we will see more and more clearly that God's will is good. It is good within itself, good without any mixture of evil in its content. It is also good for us. One of the most basic elements in my philosophy of life, if I can dignify it by calling it a "philosophy," is the conviction that God's will is always best for me and for you. This is true of his will in every area of our lives. This means, among other things, that you and I should seek to know the will of God and once knowing it, we should joyfully do it. His will is our way of happiness, usefulness, fulfillment. It is not bad medicine, as some seem to think, that finally has to be taken. If it is medicine at all, it is good medicine.

There is a sense in which our relation to the will of God is frequently like the stained-glass window of a great church building or cathedral. As we look at the window from the outside it looks dirty and dingy. We see little if any beauty in it. But once we are on the inside of the building with the sun shining through we can see the beauty and imagery of the window. It is seen as a work of art. Frequently, the will of God from the outside looks dark and foreboding. But once we step inside we see its beauty and its meaning. The one who lives the transformed or transfigured life stands on the inside of the will of God. He sees with increasing clarity that the will of God which is perfect or complete is also good.

# CHAPTER III

# The Unified Life

*For he is our peace, who has made us both one and has broken down the dividing wall of hostility.*
—Ephesians 2:14

This is the key or central verse in a more extended passage that sets forth the unity of Jew and Gentile (vv. 11–22). That unity was achieved through their union with Christ. Need I remind you that the general subject for this series of studies is "Real Life in Christ"?

Since we will study a rather extended passage, it will be helpful if you have a Bible or a New Testament open before you. The passage begins with Paul's familiar and often used "therefore" (v. 11). This "therefore" refers back to verses 1–10. In those verses Paul had described the salvation that had come to the Ephesians. They had been made alive through their union with Christ (vv. 1,5). They had been raised up with him and made to sit "in the heavenly places in Christ Jesus" (v. 6). Notice the "in Christ Jesus." (Why not check the number of times Paul used "in Christ," "in Christ Jesus" in the Ephesian letter?)

Paul pointedly said that this salvation, with all its

attendant blessings, was the work of God's grace (vv. 5–10). The greatness of that grace "should incline them to think of the past from which they have been delivered" (Expositors'). Their past condition, morally and spiritually, was in marked contrast to the present blessings they had in Christ.

They, "Gentiles in the flesh" or "Gentiles by birth" (TEV), were in contempt called "the uncircumcision by what is called the circumcision." The latter, that set the Jews apart, was "made in the flesh by hands."

Paul elsewhere says that "in Christ Jesus neither circumcision nor uncircumcision is of any avail, but faith working through love" (Gal. 5:6). In contrast to the circumcision "made in the flesh by hands," there was and is a circumcision "of the heart, spiritual and not literal" (Rom. 2:29). Paul also said that those who were "the true circumcision" worship God, glory in Christ, "and put no confidence in the flesh" (Phil. 3:3). Within the circle of true or spiritual circumcision, human distinctions based on class, color, or condition of life blend into an enriched fellowship in and for Christ.

### The Former Disunity

Previously Paul had spoken of the moral degradation of the Gentiles. In verse 12 of this passage he asked them to remember their former spiritual condition. Uncircumcision may have been and was a "fancied inferiority," but the Gentiles in the past had suffered some very real disadvantages. Paul appealed to them to remember those disadvantages. If they would do so it would give them a deeper appreciation for the blessings that had come to them in Christ. What was true for the Ephesians will also be true for you and me.

The first element in the dark picture of their past condition that Paul asked them to remember was that they "were at that time separated from Christ," or "were living utterly apart from Christ" (TLB). This was a general statement of their former condition. The other things he mentioned evolved from this separation: "The four predicates which follow give, as it were, an outline in detail of what this separation involved" (*Interpreter's*).

Being separated from Christ, the Gentiles, including the Ephesians, were "alienated from the commonwealth of Israel." They did not have the privileges and advantages of the chosen people of God. They were an alien or foreign people without the rights of citizenship: "you were foreigners" (TEV) or "utter strangers to God's chosen community" (Phillips).

Furthermore, separated from Christ and aliens or foreigners, they were "strangers to the covenants of promise." Notice the plural: "covenants." The reference is to the various covenants God made with his people through Abraham, Isaac, Jacob, Moses, David, Solomon, and others. These were covenants "of promise" or "of the promise" (Vincent). *The New English Bible* translates the statement as follows: "Outside God's covenants and the promise that goes with them." The promise which was an integral part of the covenants was ultimately fulfilled in the coming of Christ as the Messiah. The Gentiles were ignorant of and did not share in those covenants with their promise of the Messiah.

Being strangers to the covenants of promise they

had no hope. This could refer to no hope in the Messiah and hence without hope of immortality, but it also might mean no hope of any kind. Which is correct makes little difference. If one is without hope in Christ, he is, in the truest and deepest sense, without hope, period.

They were also "without God in the world." Really, they were without hope because they were without God. The word *atheos* is found only here in the New Testament. Our "atheist" is derived directly from it. There are three possible interpretations: (1) ignorant of God, (2) denying God, or (3) forsaken by God. The first is preferable; the Gentiles were ignorant of the God of the Jews, the sovereign God of the universe. They had many gods but they did not have the presence and help of the God who loves and cares in the midst of the problems and pressures of the world. To be without God in the world is like being in a wilderness without a guide or adrift at sea without a compass or a pilot. This is the situation of any person at any time who is "separated from Christ."

### The Present Unity

Beginning with verse 13, Paul painted a drastically different picture. "But now," a frequent and favorite expression of Paul's, introduces the contrast of the present with the past. The "but now" is in contrast to "at that time" (v. 12). At that time they were "separated from Christ," but now they are "in Christ Jesus" or "belong to Christ Jesus" (TLB). In the past they were far off (see Isa. 57:19), but now they "have been brought near in the blood of Christ." The definite article "the" should be inserted before Christ (*the*

Christ). This gives it "its full messianic significance" (Interpreter's).

"At that time" there had been a wall of hostility between Jew and Gentile. Now in Christ that wall or barrier had been broken down. The wall, fence, or balustrade that Paul referred to evidently was the wall or barrier in the Temple between the outer court of the Gentiles and the courts of the Jews: the court of women, of Jews in general, of priests, and the holy place. Josephus says that there were signs, some in Greek and some "in Roman letters" that " 'no foreigner should go within that sanctuary.' " One of those signs in Greek was discovered during excavation at the site of the Temple in 1871. It reads as follows: "No man of another race is to proceed within the partition and enclosing wall about the sanctuary; and anyone arrested there will have himself to blame for the penalty of death which will be imposed as a consequence" (*Interpreter's*).

Paul had a good reason to be acquainted with the restrictions concerning Gentiles in the Temple area. On one occasion it almost cost him his life. One of the charges of the Jews against him at that time was that he had brought Greeks into the Temple and thus had defiled the "holy place."

They had seen Trophimus, the Ephesian, with Paul, and they supposed that Paul had brought him into the temple (Acts 21:28–29).

Christ broke down the wall that divided Gentile from Jew "by abolishing . . . the law of commandments and ordinances" ("the law with its rules and regulations," NEB). "The rules and regulations put up the fence; but love moved it. Jesus removed the fences between man and man because he abolished all religion that is founded on rules and regulations, and brought to men a religion whose foundation is love" (Barclay). Whatever may be the walls or barriers that separate men "before Christ the barriers were up; after Christ the barriers were down. Before Christ there was no hope of unity; in Christ the new unity has come" (Barclay).

We still have walls of hostility that divide or separate us: class versus class, nation versus nation, color versus color, and even church versus church. We have the Berlin Wall, the Bamboo Curtain, and the Iron Curtain. If we had the eyes to see and the mind to comprehend we would understand that all the walls that separate us into contending camps have been broken down or abolished by the living Christ. All we have to do, which is not as simple as it sounds, is to make a reality of that which has been made a very meaningful potentiality. From God's perspective peace has been made (v. 15). Antagonizing camps have been reconciled to God and to the degree that that reconciliation is a living achievement there will be peace among men, a "peace without victory." Such reconciliation brings "hostility to an end" (v. 16), not only hostility between God and man but also between man and man. "Reconciliation with God involves and necessitates reconciliation with man" (Barclay).

Glance through verses 11–18 and notice how many times Paul used "one," which stresses the unity that has been achieved: "has made us both one" (v. 14); "one new man" (v. 15)—"It was something new, the old distinctions between Jew and Gentile being lost in a third order of 'man'—the Christian man" (Expositors'); ''one body'' (v. 16); and all of this has been achieved ''in one Spirit'' (v. 18). The oneness that Paul was talking about was between Jew and Gentile. What human divisions would he use if he were writing today? Might it be employer and employee, Russian and American, white and black? Whatever the basis of the division, we do know that ''the unity which Jesus achieves is not achieved by blotting out all the racial and national characteristics, it is achieved by making all men of all nations into Christians'' (Barclay).

## How Achieved

Now, how is this unity achieved? Let us simply list some of the statements and then discuss two or three of them. The means for the achievement of this unity of Jew and Gentile and of other divergent human groups is ''in Christ Jesus'' (v. 13), ''in the blood'' (v. 13), ''in his flesh'' (v. 15), ''in himself'' (v. 15), ''through the cross'' (v. 16), ''through him'' (v. 15). These leave no doubt about who (1) has broken down the dividing wall of hostility, (2) has abolished the law of commandments and ordinances, (3) has created one new man in place of the two, (4) has made peace between contending forces, (5) has reconciled both to God, (6) has preached peace to those far off as well as those near, and (7) made it possible for both Jew and Gentile and all of us to have access ''in one Spirit to the Father.''

Let us notice two or three of the specific statements above. ''In his flesh'' (v. 15) evidently refers primarily to Christ's death on the cross. In other connections we have references to ''in the blood of Christ'' (v.

13) and "through the cross" (v. 16). Some interpret "in his flesh" to include his participation in the life of humanity (Interpreter's).

Notice that it is "in himself" (v. 15) and not "by" or "through" himself. The two, Jew and Gentile, come together or are "fused . . . together" (TLB) through their union in him. It is in this way alone that the two can become "one new man" ("person," TLB).

Let us note in particular that "he is our peace" (v. 14). The emphasis is on *he*. He alone is our peace. He himself, and not just or primarily what he did. "He is our peace with God and so with each other" (Robertson). He brought "the hostility to an end." How? By reconciling "us both to God in one body through the cross" (v. 16), "and he came and preached peace to you who were far off [the Gentiles] and peace to those who were near [the Jews]" (v. 17). This might refer to preaching by Jesus during his earthly ministry or in his post-resurrection appearances, but it seems more likely that it refers primarily to "his coming in His Spirit. It was preaching through the apostles and others that had changed the status of these Gentile Christians" (*Expositors'*).

One evidence that peace between warring parties has been attained and also a factor in that attainment is the fact that through Christ both Jew and Gentile have "access in one Spirit to the Father" (v. 18). The word "access" contains a very beautiful and meaningful concept. It is the word that is used for an introduction to a prominent person such as an ambassador or even a king. It suggests "the high privilege of admission to the presence of a glorious monarch. Christ brings us into the throne room of the King of kings and causes

us to know him in the fulness of his glory as Father"
(Interpreter's). In other words, the way is open into
the holy of holies. The veil or curtain of the Temple
has been torn in two. In Christ, not only Jew and
Gentile but all men of every class and color have direct
access to the Father. What a glorious privilege: we
have been introduced to our heavenly Father. Williams
translates the verse as follows: "For it is by Him
through one Spirit that both of us now have an introduction to the Father." Peter, using the same word, says,
"For Christ also died for sins once for all, the righteous
for the unrighteous, that he might bring us to God
[introduce us to God or provide for us access to God]"
(1 Pet. 3:18). Let us repeat the glorious truth that this
access is available to all—to you, to me, to all men.
When we come to Christ we also come into the presence of his Father and our Father.

## Conclusion

What might be considered a summary or a conclusion
to Paul's statement concerning the unity in Christ of
Jew and Gentile is introduced with "so then" (v. 19)
or "then" (NEB). Here again is the "therefore" perspective. Let us note in somewhat summary fashion
what Paul suggested to the Ephesians.

Previously they had been alienated from the commonwealth of Israel, and were strangers to the covenants of promise (v. 12), but now through their union
with Christ they "are no longer strangers and
sojourners" ("aliens in a foreign land," NEB). Now
they are "fellow-citizens of God's people and members
of His family" (v. 19, Williams). The door into the
family of God is open to all who will come through

faith in Christ. "It is the tragedy of the church that it is so often more exclusive than God" (Barclay).

Paul then shifted from the picture or symbol of the family to that of a building. The family or household of God is built upon the foundation not only of the apostles but also the prophets. It is particularly important to remember that Christ is "the chief cornerstone": "the stone placed at the summit of the edifice as its crown and completion" (*Interpreter's*). There is no doubt that "He is the one who holds the whole building together and makes it grow into a sacred temple in the Lord" (v. 21, TEV), "a beautiful, constantly growing temple for God" (TLB). The unity in the Christian fellowship of Jew and Gentile and all other human divisions is the work of the indwelling Christ. Paul further says, "In union with him you two are being built together with all others into a house where God lives through his Spirit" (v. 22, TEV).

Notice "built" (v. 20) and "are built" or "are being built" (TEV). This points up again a persistent paradox in the Christian experience: the Gentiles or Ephesians had been "built upon the foundation" that had been laid: they were also "being built together with all the others." Here is past fact coupled with present reality and by implication with future hope. Past fact, present reality, and future hope all stem from and are dependent upon our union with the resurrected Christ. He is the hope of unity within our own lives, of unity between different human groups, and of unity in the church or Christian fellowship.

### Application

If Paul were writing his epistles to contemporary

churches, he would doubtlessly apply his basic concepts to contemporary problems. We do not have the Gentile-Jewish problem, at least not in the sense and to the degree that it was present in New Testament days. But we do have class and racial divisions of comparable seriousness. Let us apply what Paul said concerning the unity that was available in Christ to the race problem.

Some problems in the area of race can be solved by laws and by the courts. This has been and is true, to a large degree, of segregation in our society on the basis of race or color. The walls of segregation are being broken down. These walls, however, may be largely eliminated and yet no meaningful integration take place.

There still remain "walls of hostility" in the hearts of many people. There are even "walls of hostility" in many churches as sharp as any that ever existed in the Temple. These walls of hostility in the temple of God (his church) can be broken down only by the spirit of the crucified and risen Christ as he dwells in the midst of his people.

Furthermore, the walls of prejudice that so many of us—black, brown, and white—have erected in our hearts will be broken down only as we let the risen Christ live in us and express himself through us.

A few years ago when the segregation pattern was still in force in the Deep South, "Brother Clem," a Yugoslav Baptist pastor, visited the United States. He himself told of an experience he had in traveling by bus from Alabama to North Carolina. When he got on the bus, all the seats toward the front were taken. He took a seat by a Negro woman near the rear of the bus. He sat reading his paper but shortly he heard a buzzing that got louder. A young white man came over, took him by his tie, and practically lifting him out of his seat, said, "What do you mean sitting by this nigger?"

The bus driver pulled the bus to the side of the road and asked everyone to be seated. He came back toward where Brother Clem was. He told the folks on the bus that Brother Clem did not know the customs of our society. He explained that Brother Clem shared with him as he got on the bus that he was a Baptist pastor from Yugoslavia.

When the bus driver mentioned that Clem was a Baptist, the old Negro lady by whom he had been seated, with a smile that creased her wrinkled face, reached out her hand and said, "The Lord bless you, brother. I am a Baptist too." He said that a young black man with his white teeth shining and a smile upon his face stepped from the back seat of the bus and reached out his hand saying, "Thank the Lord, I am a Baptist too." Then the young white man who had practically lifted him out of his seat came with his face as white as his shirt and said, "I apologize to you. Will you forgive me? I am a Baptist too."

Brother Clem said the bus driver turned to him and asked, "What do you suggest that we do now?" Clem's reply was, "I would like for us to sing one of my favorite hymns," to which the bus driver replied, "You start and we will join you."

Brother Clem started and others joined him in singing:

Amazing grace! how sweet the sound,
That saved a wretch like me!
I once was lost, but now am found,
Was blind, but now I see.

Clem said, "We went down the highway a singing congregation." It is only the grace of God as expressed in and through his Son that will make it possible for all of God's children to become *one* singing congregation.

Let us close by reading two verses of this passage from Ephesians from Phillips' translation. Every translation is an interpretation, none more so than Phillips'. He does, however, frequently make a passage take on new life. His translation of verses 16 and 17 is as follows: "For he reconciled both to God by the sacrifice of one body on the cross, and by this act made utterly irrelevant the antagonism between them. Then he came and told both you who were far from God and us who were near that the war was over."

Wouldn't it be wonderful if Christians of every class and race would recognize that their antagonism is "utterly irrelevant" and that "the war is over"? This will be true to the degree that we let the spirit of the resurrected Christ find expression in us and through us.

# CHAPTER IV

# The Worthy Life

*I therefore, a prisoner for the Lord, beg you to lead a life worthy of the calling to which you have been called.*—Ephesians 4:1

Review in your mind the preceding discussions. It has been suggested that we have been made new creations in Christ Jesus. Since this is true we should not be conformed to this world. We should be transformed and as a result be a transforming influence in the world. In the immediate preceding discussion it was suggested that through our union with Christ we are made *one.* Human differences and distinctions blend into one fellowship in Christ. In the present study, also from the Ephesian letter, it is suggested that all of us, which includes those of various racial and culture groups who have been made one in Christ, should live a life worthy of the calling to which we have been called.

Similar to Paul's appeal in Romans to live the transformed life, his appeal here in Ephesians to live the worthy life stands at the beginning of the practical portion of the epistle. Also, as in Romans, the word "therefore" is used to make the transition from the more theological to the more practical. The word "more," in the preceding sentence, is necessary since there is some mixing of the theological and the ethical or practical in both sections of the epistle. For example, our discussion of "The Unified Life" in the preceding chapter was based on a study of Ephesians 2:11–22, in the theological portion of the epistle.

Notice, however, that in Ephesians the break between the more theological and more practical is somewhat sharper than usual. Paul closed the first three chapters with a doxology (3:20–21). Let me suggest again that the logical order is: Christian doctrine followed by Christian conduct. Christian morality is "therefore morality."

These devotional messages are on the general title "Real Life in Christ." Check the first three chapters of Ephesians and notice how many times Paul uses "in Christ," "in Christ Jesus," "in Jesus Christ," and "in him."

In introducing his appeal to the Ephesians to walk worthy (KJV) or to live a worthy life, Paul referred to himself as "a prisoner for the Lord," or literally "in the Lord" and possibly meaning because he was in the Lord. At least, even in prison he was "in the Lord." The fact that he was a prisoner gave added strength to his appeal but it was not the basis or motive for the appeal. No, his exhortation was grounded in what Paul had said previously concerning the grace and goodness of God. "Christian moral goodness is thanksgiving goodness" (*Interpreter's*).

### The Exhortation

Notice again that Paul, as in Romans 12:1, did not command but begged, beseeched (KJV), entreated

(NEB), or urged (TEV) the Ephesians. Also notice the content of his urging or exhortation: "to lead a life worthy of the calling to which you have been called." The word (*peripateo*) translated "lead a life," "live a life" (TEV), or "walk" (KJV) literally means to walk around or about. We get our English word "peripatetic" from it: a peripatetic teacher is one who moves from place to place. Jesus was such a teacher. With only two or three exceptions the word is translated "walk" in the King James Version. The Revised Standard Version sometimes translates it "lead a life" as here but also frequently translates it "walk."

A study of the word "walk" would be a very interesting and rewarding experience. It is used in the figurative sense quite often in both Testaments. The Old Testament speaks of God going with Israel (Ex. 33:16; Deut. 20:4). In turn, his people were to walk with him (Mic. 6:8) or before him (Ps. 116:9) righteously (Isa. 33:15), in faithfulness (Isa. 38:3), and in peace (Mal. 2:6). Particularly interesting from our perspective is the frequent admonition for the people of God to walk in the way of the Lord (see Deut. 8:6; 10:12; 28:9; 2 Kings 21:22).

The term "walk" or "live," depending on the version used, is particularly prevalent in the Pauline and Johannine writings. The following are a few of many possible examples from Paul's epistles: He admonished the Romans to walk in newness of life (Rom. 6:4). They should not walk after or according to the flesh but "according to the Spirit" (Rom. 8:4). To the Corinthians he said, "We walk by faith, not by sight" (2 Cor. 5:7). He suggested that the Galatians "walk by the Spirit" (Gal. 5:16, 25) and that the Thessalonians "lead a life worthy of God" or "walk worthy of God" (1 Thess. 2:12, KJV) and to live or walk so as to please God (1 Thess. 4:1). A particularly challenging statement is the following by John: "He who says he abides in him ought to walk in the same way in which he walked" (1 John 2:6). Where would the footsteps of Jesus take us if we walked "in the same way in which he walked"? We would walk the way of helpful, unselfish service. We would go about doing good. Ultimately we would walk with him into the garden of Gethsemane, up Calvary, into the tomb, and then, thank the Lord, out of the tomb.

The word *peripateo* is found more frequently (seven times) in Ephesians than in any other of Paul's epistles. All but two of these references are in the practical section of the epistle (chaps. 4—6). A particularly important reference is in the theological portion of the epistle. After he had said that we are saved by grace through faith, not of works, he added: "For we are his workmanship, created in Christ Jesus for good works, which God prepared beforehand, that we should walk in them" (Eph. 2:10).

What is the "calling" or "vocation" (KJV) referred to in Ephesians 4:1? Is it the initial Christian experience when we became children of God? Or, does it refer to a special call to perform some distinctive function for the Lord, his church, and his people? It could refer to either but it seems logical to conclude that Paul was referring to the call to be a Christian.

We refer to the initial Christian experience as "conversion" or a "profession of faith." Looked at from the divine perspective, it is a call. *Today's English Version* translates the latter portion of verse 1 as follows: "live a life that measures up to the standard God set when he called you."

What was and is that standard? Will you not agree that the standard is to be like the One with whom we have been brought into union? Or, as Paul expressed it elsewhere, we are to "press toward the mark ["goal"] for the prize of the high calling ["upward call"] of God in Christ Jesus" (Phil. 3:14, KJV). To be like him is life's highest calling.

## Qualities of the Worthy Life

Barclay suggests that these verses (Eph. 4:1–3) "shine with words which are like jewels." Two of these jewel-like words have already been mentioned, "walk" or "live" and "calling." Paul was not satisfied, however, with a general exhortation to the Ephesians to live a life worthy of their calling. In some additional "words which are like jewels" he spelled out some of the specific qualities that would characterize a worthy life. This is not a complete listing. Many others are mentioned elsewhere in the Pauline epistles.

The first quality or character trait mentioned is *lowliness* or *humility*. It is opposite to pride or a haughty spirit. The word translated lowliness or humility was used very little before the coming of Christ and then always in a bad sense. As a virtue "humility" is distinctly an outgrowth of the gospel.

There are a number of factors that should contribute to a wholesome degree of humility. One is the awareness of our creatureliness and the limitations this place on us. Another is the conviction that our calling to be a Christian is of grace. Then there is the glory of the calling itself. We are in the family of God. Our

Father is the sovereign God of the universe. We are his and he through the Spirit lives within us. How glorious this is but also how unworthy we are of this rich and blessed privilege!

Another factor that contributes to our humility is the continuing sense of sin and the need for forgiveness. There are times when we feel like crying out with Paul: "Christ Jesus came into the world to save sinners; of whom I am chief" (1 Tim. 1:15, KJV). Notice not "was chief" but "am chief." If Paul felt that way, how much more this should be true of you and me!

William Barclay says that "Christian humility comes from setting life beside the life of Christ and in the light of the demands of God." Updating the golfers mentioned, Barclay suggests that one might consider himself a good golfer until he has seen Palmer, Nicklaus, or Trevino. When we measure ourselves by the stature of Christ, we feel like saying with the publican or tax collector, "God, be merciful to me a sinner!" (Luke 18:13).

What about the quality of humility? Do we have it? To what degree? It should be remembered that if we are too conscious of our humility that very fact may be an evidence that we are not humble. There is a considerable element of self-forgetfulness in humility. We should also remember that lowliness or humility applies to our relations with our fellowman as well as with God. Paul admonished the Philippians, "In humility count others better than yourselves" (Phil. 2:3).

A second characteristic of the worthy life mentioned here is *meekness* or *gentleness* (NASB, and most modern translations). Notice that it is connected with humility with an "and." The two are very closely related. As suggested above, humility is the opposite of pride; meekness or gentleness is the opposite of self-assertion.

Paul entreated the Corinthians "by the meekness and gentleness of Christ" (2 Cor. 10:1). Jesus spoke of himself as "gentle and lowly in heart" (Matt. 11:29). Gentleness is a fruit of the Spirit (Gal. 5:23). The "man of God" should "aim at righteousness, godliness, faith, love, steadfastness, gentleness" (1 Tim. 6:11). The Lord's servant must correct "his opponents with gentleness" (2 Tim. 2:25). Paul instructed Titus "to be gentle, and to show perfect courtesy toward all men" (Titus 3:2). The Galatians were told to restore one who had been "overtaken in any trespass . . . in a spirit of gentleness" (Gal. 6:1). Peter said that we should be prepared to make a defense of our faith but to "do it with gentleness and reverence" (1 Pet. 3:15).

Another characteristic of the worthy life specifically spelled out is *patience* or *long-suffering* (KJV). The New Testament speaks of the patience of God. For example, Paul said that God had "endured with much patience the vessels of wrath made for destruction" (Rom. 9:22). Peter said that "God's patience waited in the days of Noah" (1 Pet. 3:20). "God's patience waits and loves" (Barclay). Do we have the patience that "waits and loves"?

After Paul had said that "Christ Jesus came into the world to save sinners, and I am the foremost of sinners," he added: "but I received mercy for this reason, that in me, as the foremost, Jesus Christ might display his perfect ["full," TEV] patience for an example to those who were to believe in him for eternal life" (1 Tim. 1:15–16).

Notice the words "for an example." Here, as in every area of life, the child of God is never asked to do or be something that Jesus did not fully demonstrate in his own life. Ours cannot be "perfect patience" but we can have increasing patience as we walk in union with the resurrected Christ. We are to be patient in our relations with one another as God has been and is patient toward us. One who is patient refuses to strike back, to retaliate. What an example our Lord set for us: "When he was reviled ["cursed," TEV], he did not revile in return; when he suffered, he did not threaten." Then notice the secret to such a spirit of patience and nonretaliation: "but he trusted to him who justly judges" (1 Pet. 2:23).

It was Paul who said that "love is patient and kind" (1 Cor. 13:4). Both of these marvelous virtues (love and patience) are the fruit of the Spirit (Gal. 5:22) and the product of the resurrected life (Col. 3:12, 14). Timothy was exhorted to "be unfailing in patience and in teaching" (2 Tim. 4:2) or "teaching with all patience" (TEV). As one who has taught most of his life I can testify that it requires considerable patience.

Another quality or characteristic of the worthy life, which is close akin to patience, is *forbearance:* "forbearing one another in love." Phillips says, "making allowances for each other because you love each other." We need to make allowances for one another even and possibly especially within the Christian fellowship. Entirely too many of us are offended more easily by something that happens within our church fellowship than we would be if the same thing happened elsewhere. All of us are in need of forbearance. In

turn, we should be forbearing. There are few thing
that will add more to our effectiveness in the Lord'
work than to be able to work with people as they are
This will require considerable forbearance but no mor
than it will require for others to work with us.

One thing that should help us to be forbearing i
to remember that the Lord has had to forgive and over
look much more in us than we will ever have to forbea
or overlook in any fellow Christian. It may be wel
for us to remember a statement that an old professo
of mine once made. His statement was: "The Lor
can hit some mighty straight licks with crooked sticks."
If he could not, he would not hit many straight licks

As is true of every other quality or Christian virtue
forbearance finds its fullest expression in God. Pau
joined forbearance with kindness and patience as qual
ities of God (Rom. 2:4). He also spoke of "divin
forbearance" (Rom. 3:25).

Paul admonished the Philippians to "let all me
know your forbearance" (Phil. 4:5). He joined forbear
ance and forgiveness in his letter to the Colossians
"Put on then, as God's chosen ones, holy and belov
ed, compassion, kindness, lowliness, meekness an
patience, forbearing one another and, if one has
complaint against another, forgiving each other; as th
Lord has forgiven you, so you also must forgive"
(Col. 3:12–13). Here is both motive and pattern o
model—"as the Lord."

Another mark of the worthy life is *love* (*agape*). "I
love" may be attached only to forbearance but it seem
reasonable to believe that the words were meant t
be related to all the preceding qualities. At least w
know that they are possible only in love. "Love i

basic attitude of seeking the highest good of others, and it will therefore lead to all these qualities and include them all" (*Tyndale*). Paul had prayed that the Ephesians might be "rooted and grounded in love" (Eph. 3:17). He admonished them to "speak the truth in love" (Eph. 4:15). Here he suggested that if they had the qualities of humility, gentleness, and forbearance "in love" they would be leading a life worthy of their calling. The emphasis was placed on love by stating it last.

How do we measure up? How much are these qualities of a worthy life evident in our lives?

### Motive

Now, let us notice verse 3: "eager to maintain the unity of the Spirit in the bond of peace." Some treat this verse as another quality or virtue along with humility, gentleness, forbearance, and love. We prefer to consider it the motive for the worthy life. At least, we know that there can be no lasting unity within the Christian fellowship without the virtues or qualities previously mentioned. There is a sense in which they are both the products of and at the same time conditions for unity within that fellowship. In commenting on verse 3, it has been suggested that the remainder of the letter may be considered an expression of the appeal that had been made in verses 1 and 2: the unity of the Spirit is the first particular in this expansion (*Tyndale*).

There was urgency expressed in the appeal: "eager," "spare no effort" (NEB), "make haste" (Vincent), "continuing with eager earnestness" (Williams). These suggest "a blazing zeal" (*In-*

*terpreter's*). They were to be eager "to maintain" or "to preserve" (*International*), which suggests that what they were admonished to maintain or preserve was already in their possession.

The unity of which Paul spoke was the unity of the Spirit. In the great section on unity, discussed in the preceding chapter of this book, Paul spoke of "one new man" (v. 15), "one body" (v. 16), and "one Spirit" (v. 18). The oneness there, as in this chapter (4), is achieved in and by the Spirit. The Ephesians could not and no Christian or group of Christians can create that unity. The divine Spirit produces it. We should seek to maintain or preserve it. One way we can do that is to live a life worthy of our calling as Christians: a life of humility, gentleness, forbearance, and love. Another way we can preserve or guard the unity the Spirit gives is to be at peace with one another: "Peace is the bond in which the unity is kept" (*International*).

This "peace" is not external and formal but internal and real. First and basically it is peace with God and that inevitably moves us toward peace with our fellowman. Just as love for God and fellowman belong together, so peace with God and man belong together. Here is one of the great paradoxes of the Scriptures: Peace is a product or fruit of the Spirit (Gal. 5:22); it is also a condition for the Spirit's presence and the unity that he gives.

### Conclusion

The walk or life of the Christian was a continuing emphasis of Paul in the Ephesian letter. In the fifth chapter, he exhorted the Ephesians to "walk in love" or "practice living in love" (v. 2, Williams), to "walk as children of light" (v. 8), and to look carefully how they walked (v. 15). It is the same word (*peripateo*) translated "lead a life" in 4:1.

Notice the opening exhortation of chapter 5: "Therefore be imitators of God," "Keep on following God's example" (Williams). One area in which we should imitate or follow him is in regard to love. We should "walk in love, as Christ loved us and gave himself up for us." Here again Christ provides both pattern and motive.

Another way that we can walk or live worthy of our calling is to walk as children of light. It was Jesus who said that we are the light of the world. Ours is not a reflected light like the moon. No, ours is a light from within. The fruit of such a light "is found in all that is good and right and true" (5:9). Williams translates the verse as follows: "You must live like children of light, for the product of light consists in practicing everything that is good and right and true."

Again Paul said, "Look carefully, then, how you walk, not as unwise but as wise" (5:15) or "pay close attention to how you live" (TEV). This is a further description of the worthy walk or life.

Let us close by turning to a couple of verses in Colossians, an epistle closely related and strikingly similar to Ephesians. Paul prayed for the Colossians that they might "lead a life worthy ["walk worthy," KJV] of the Lord, fully pleasing to him, bearing fruit in every good work and increasing in the knowledge of God" (Col. 1:10).

A life worthy of the Lord
    will be pleasing to him
    will bear fruit for him

will increase in the knowledge of him.

On the other hand, "increasing in the knowledge of God" will increase our fruit for God and will enable us increasingly to lead a life worthy of one who is in the family of God.

What a challenge there is in another word of Paul to the Colossians: "Since you have accepted Christ Jesus as Lord, live in union with him. Keep your roots deep in him, build your lives on him, and become ever stronger in your faith, as you were taught. And be filled with thanksgiving" (Col. 2:6–7, TEV).

Equally challenging is Paul's admonition to the Philippians: "Let your manner of life be worthy of the gospel of Christ" (Phil. 1:27). Let us pray that that will increasingly be true of each of us!

# CHAPTER V

# The Mature Life

*And his gifts were that some should be apostles . . . for the equipment of the saints, . . . until we all attain . . . to mature manhood, to the measure of the stature of the fulness of Christ.*—Ephesians 4:11–13

Through our union with Christ, we have been made new creations in Christ Jesus. At that time we were babes in Christ, but we were not supposed to remain babes. Will you not agree, however, that entirely too many of us are still babes or at best we are adolescent in our spiritual development and perspective when we should be mature men and women in and for Christ? Too many of us still have to be fed a milk diet when, to use a Pauline expression, we should be mature enough for solid food (1 Cor. 3:2). Many of us who have been Christians long enough to be teachers of others are still, as the writer of Hebrews said, in need of others to teach us the first principles of our faith. Similar to Paul, the author concluded that "solid food is for the mature, for those who have their faculties trained by practice to distinguish good from evil" (Heb. 5:14). Are we that mature?

We are admonished in the Scriptures to "grow in

the grace and knowledge of our Lord and Savior Jesus Christ" (2 Pet. 3:18). Regardless of how mature we may be, we are in need of that exhortation.

## The Measure of Our Maturity

Many scholars suggest that these verses from Ephesians, the third of our studies from this one epistle, refer to the growth or maturity of the church as the body of Christ. The building up of the body of Christ is clearly the comprehensive goal of the work of the specially gifted or called ones along with all the saints. The "building up of the body of Christ" may include growth in members or numbers but primarily growth in maturity.

The church as the body of Christ cannot be built up or attain maturity except as individual members of that body mature or grow. As Mackay says, "To build up the Body of Christ and to achieve Christian maturity are inseparably related" (p. 158). The individual Christian cannot mature apart from the body while the body cannot mature except as individuals mature. There is set forth in these verses the ultimate goal or standard for the maturity of the individual child of God as well as for the church as the body of Christ.

The most challenging portion of this entire passage, from the perspective of our study, is the last part of verse 13. The body of Christ is to be built up "until we all attain . . . to mature manhood, to the measure of the stature of the fullness of Christ." Different translations shed some additional light on these challenging words. *The New English Bible* translates the passage as follows: "To mature manhood, measured by nothing less than the full stature of Christ"; while Williams says: "to a mature manhood and to a perfect measure of Christ's moral stature." The fullness spoken of is "that which belongs to Christ and is imparted by Him" (Vincent). It has also been suggested that the fullness referred to is "the sum of the qualities which make Him what He is . . . and when these are in us we shall have reached our maturity and attained to the goal set before us" (*Expositors'*).

Regardless of the correct translation, the idea of perfection is present. This is certainly true since our maturity is to be measured by "nothing less than the full stature of Christ," by the "perfect measure of Christ's moral stature," or by "the sum of the qualities which make Him what He is." He lived a perfect life. He was fully mature or complete in every way.

We should not measure our maturity by the lives of neighbors, friends, loved ones, fellow church members, or even by the best Christians we know. The measure of our maturity is "the stature which belongs to the fullness of Christ" (NASB). Here is an ideal beyond our attainment in this life, but one that should challenge us to the end of life's journey. It should give us an abiding sense of humility and of dependence upon our heavenly Father.

Paul also emphasized the mature life in verse 15. He said, "Speaking the truth in love, we are to grow up in every way ["in all respects," NASB] into him ["growing up into perfect union with Him," Williams] who is the head, into Christ." We were brought into union with the resurrected Christ in our initial Christian experience. That experience which made us new creations in Christ was deeply satisfying, but paradoxically the more fully we understand it the deeper is our dissatisfaction with ourselves. This dissatisfaction stems from the fact that we see increasingly how far short we fall of doing what we ought to do and particularly of being what we ought to be for him and in him. We are to grow up into perfect union with him. This growth is "into" or "unto" Christ—"Christ the Head being the *end* and *object* of the growth of the members" (*Expositors'*). This is another ideal of perfection which we shall not attain until we awake in his likeness. This growth into or unto Christ is to be "in every way" or "in all respects"; which expresses the extent or scope of the growth.

When measured by the stature found in Christ, *how tall are we?* What is our stature in the home, in the church, where we work, and in the world in general? Let us ask an additional question: If we are not as mature as we should be, and if we are not maturing as rapidly as we should, why is this true? Honest answers to these questions can be tremendously significant for each one of us.

Our stature for Christ is dependent on how deep we have gone with him. A friend of a back-yard gardener was teasing him about the small size of his garden. The gardener said, "I know my garden is not very long and it is not very wide, but it is four thousand miles deep." How deep have we gone? Our depth will determine our fruitfulness for God.

### The Evidences of Our Maturity

The fact that the ultimate goal of Christian maturity is far beyond our present level of living should not discourage but challenge us. The real test of our lives is not whether or not we have attained full maturity, but whether or not we are maturing. Are we more mature today than yesterday? this week than last week? this month than last month? this year than last year? In other words, the real test of our lives is the direction of our lives. Are we moving toward maturity measured by the fullness that belongs to Christ?

How can we determine whether or not we are maturing? There are many proofs or evidences. The Ephesian passages suggest some purposes of maturity—"so that" (v. 14). If those purposes are fulfilled in our lives, then we have the evidences or the proofs of maturity. Since we never measure up fully, possibly it should be said: "To the degree that these purposes are fulfilled in our lives, to that degree we have the evidences of spiritual maturity."

Paul specifically suggested that if we are mature, we will no longer be like children "tossed to and fro and carried about with every wind of doctrine," "every chance wind of teaching" (Phillips), or "every fresh gust of teaching" (NEB). The picture or metaphor here is of a ship adrift at sea at the mercy of the waves. If we are mature, we shall not be tossed about. In other words, the mature person is a stable person. One can depend on him. One does not have to wonder what his decision will be, what stand he will take on any great moral or religious issue. Also, his roots will be deep enough to enable him to ride the storms of life. The mature child of God may be battered by the storms but he will not be defeated by them.

As suggested previously, the overall purpose of the work of the specially gifted ones along with the saints in general is the building up of the body of Christ (v. 12). The remaining verses (13-16) can properly be considered an enlargement and exposition of this overall purpose. In verses 15 and 16 this building up is spelled out rather specifically. The growth or maturity of the body (1) is derived from the head, (2) is dependent on the vital union of the parts of the body with the head, and (3) on the proper relating of each part to the whole. If these conditions for growth are met, it is implied that growth will be symmetrical and will be achieved in love.

There are several things implied if not specifically suggested in verses 15 and 16 that have important significance for us in our study of the mature Christian life. Basic to all that we find there is the fact that Christ is the head not only of the church but also of each individual Christian. In turn we, as individuals, are to be rightly related to the body but supremely rightly related to Christ as the Head of the body or the church.

Let us restate in a slightly different way some of the evidences of maturity suggested by a study of these verses. First, if we are mature Christians we will recognize our dependence on the resurrected Christ, the head of the body. Our maturing comes from our union with and response to him. Another evidence of maturity will be our recognition of our dependence on and vital relationship to the body of Christ or the church. To be vitally related to Christ is to be vitally related to his church. Much of the food for growth and strength for service which comes from the resurrected Christ flows to us through his church as his body.

Another evidence of and factor in our maturity will be our relation to one another as parts of the body. We are to be "joined and knit together . . . with each part working properly." Still another evidence of our maturity and at the same time a contributor to our maturing is our recognition that we have a distinctive place to fill or part to play in the life of the body and in relation to the other parts of the body. The mature child of God will be satisfied to do his best to fulfill his own distinctive responsibility.

While we do not want to go too far afield from the particular passage of Scripture we are studying, let us list a few of the many additional evidences of moral and spiritual maturing. Among these are the following: (1) We shall be increasingly able to adjust to the inevitabilities of life. (2) We shall establish in our lives basic principles on which we shall make our decisions—our conduct will be determined more by inner principles and less by outer pressure. (3) Our faith will be based more on essentials and less on nonessentials. (4) We shall measure our own and others' religion by its vitalities more than by its formalities. (5) We shall be motivated more by love and less by fear. (6) We will be more consistently conscious of the presence of the Lord, of the leadership of the Holy Spirit in our lives, and less dependent on outstanding experiences or special occasions for our religious vitality.

## The Means for Our Maturity

It has been suggested that the ultimate standard for or measure of our maturity is the maturity found in Christ. We have also acknowledged that we have not attained and cannot fully measure up to this standard but that we should move in that direction. We have also pointed out some evidences or proofs that will indicate that we have attained some degree of maturity.

Now, let us examine some of the available means or methods that will enable us to move toward maturity. One such means or method implied in the Ephesian passage is our favorable response to the work of evangelists, pastors, teachers, and others whom the Lord has given to his church. The first stated purpose of these specially gifted ones is "the equipment of the saints" or "God's people" (NEB). The word for "perfecting" (KJV) or "equipment" (*katartismon*) comes from a root which means to mend or repair what is broken (see Matt. 4:21; Mark 1:19), or to complete what is unfinished (see Luke 6:40; Rom. 9:29). "The word is used in surgery for setting a broken limb, or for putting a joint that is out of place back into its place" (Barclay). Ethically speaking, the word means "to strengthen, perfect, complete, make one what he ought to be" (Thayer, *Greek-English Lexicon*). Whatever may be the correct translation, will you not agree that all of us need to be mended, repaired, strengthened, and made what we ought to be? This mending or repairing is to prepare us for our work of ministry. The mending or the equipping of the saints which is a process is not an end but a means to an end.

Notice that there is a comma following the word "saints." That comma does not belong there and is not found in most versions other than the King James and Revised Standard versions. It has been called "the fatal comma." Whether or not the comma is there makes a great deal of difference. If retained, then the work of the ministry and of the building up of the body of Christ as well as the equipping of the saints is the work of the apostles and other specially gifted and called ones. If the comma is eliminated, as it should be, then the basic work of the specially designated ones is to equip the saints that they in turn may minister or serve and thus contribute to the building up of the body of Christ.

Our acceptance of our personal responsibility for the ministry is in a sense a measure and an evidence of our maturity. But, at the same time, it is also a method or means for our maturing. There may be and are some from within the Christian fellowship who are uniquely called to perform distinctive functions for that fellowship. The basic call to minister or serve, however, is a call to all. We believe in the priesthood of the believer. One aspect of that priesthood has been considerably neglected. Our direct access to God without the need for a priest or intermediary has been stressed considerably. Frequently, however, the responsibility of the believer to minister to and for others has not been emphasized sufficiently. This is the other or "flip" side of the priesthood of the believer.

We should not forget that the call to us to minister or serve is not limited to a church building. The body of Christ cannot be contained within the building. The body, or the church, is any place where we and others who have been brought into union with Christ live and work. We minister just as definitely in the home, on the street, in the shop, as we do in the services of our church. If we are mature in Christian perspective we will be deeply concerned for the work of Christ in the world. The more mature we are, the broader will be our perspective concerning his work and our responsibility for it. In turn, the broadening of our perspective will be a factor in our maturing.

If we are to mature as we should, we must not only cooperate with the "functional ministers" of the church in what they seek to do for us; we must also be responsive to the inner prompting or leading of the divine Spirit. In other words, we mature more and more into the likeness of Christ by living in fellowship with him. We cannot "grow up in every way into him" or "unto him" unless we let him live in us and have his way through us. "To be 'in Christ' and to grow up into him in all things—these are complementary aspects of our lives; for our union with Christ is not a mechanical attachment which remains static, but participation in a dynamic, growing life" (*Interpreter's*).

The main thing that is needed in our lives is an inner conformity to his likeness. If this is true in our lives, there will follow inevitably the outer evidence that he lives within us. This means, among other things, that being a real Christian involves primarily a relationship, but a relationship so deeply vital and meaningful that it cannot help but influence outer conduct. The real Christian life flows from within outwards. Its basic concern is not with conduct but with character which is inner.

One verse of an old song we used to sing expresses something of the idea of inner renewal:

> Take time to be holy,
>   The world rushes on;
> Spend much time in secret
>   With Jesus alone:
> By looking to Jesus
>   Like Him thou shalt be;
> Thy friends in thy conduct
>   His likeness shall see.
>
> —W. D. LONGSTAFF

A growing likeness to Jesus may not be as simple, however, as the song suggests. Really, it is not "looking to Jesus" but it is living with and responding to the resurrected Christ that will move us toward maturity.

In conclusion, permit me to ask again: How mature are we? How tall are we when we measure ourselves by the stature of Christ? Georgia Harkness says that "in Jesus we see what God is like and what man should become." A knowledge of what Jesus was like comes to us as we study the Scriptures and meditate upon their truths. The full challenge never comes to us, however, until the living Christ not only speaks to us through the Scriptures but also in a direct way within our own hearts and lives. Have we felt, or better, do we feel the tug "of the upward call of God in Christ Jesus?" (Phil. 3:14).

If we keep in mind the fact that our maturity is to be measured by the fullness "which belongs to Christ" we will be saved from any spirit of self-righteousness, which tends to be a besetting sin of many Christians. Entirely too many of us tend to say with the Pharisee, "God, I thank thee, that I am not as other men, . . . even as this publican" (Luke 18:11, KJV). When we properly understand God's expectations of us, our reactions will be those of the publican or tax collector. He "standing afar off, would not lift up so much as his eyes unto heaven, but smote his breast saying, God be merciful to me a sinner" (Luke 18:13, KJV).

Really, the more mature we become in Christ the more conscious we shall be of our immaturity. You remember that the first reaction of Isaiah when he saw the Lord high and lifted up was, "Woe is me! for I am undone; because I am a man of unclean lips." Why did Isaiah have this conviction? He gives the reason: "For mine eyes have seen the King, the Lord of hosts" (Isa. 6:5, KJV). The first reaction of anyone who has seen the Lord, regardless of how mature he may be as a Christian, will be "Woe is me!"

When I was in college, my parents lived on a farm in the hill or ridge country of East Tennessee. The college was only about thirty miles from my home and I occasionally spent the weekend with my parents. One Friday afternoon I arrived home rather late. My mother's washing was still on the line. As usual it was spotlessly white. We were very poor, being share-croppers, but my mother frequently said, "We may not have much but we can keep clean what we have."

It had been cloudy during the day and the wash had not dried. She did an unusual thing and left her clothes on the line overnight. The next morning when I looked out the window of our one little upstairs room, everything was covered with snow. The side of the ridge was covered; the limbs of the cedars were bending under the load of the snow; the barn, the tool shed, the chicken house, and everything was covered. Now, how did my mother's wash look the next morning? You know, of course, that it no longer looked spotlessly white. It looked dingy. Why? They were the same clothes that were there the day before. The difference was that now there was something out there that was really white: snow that was touched with the white-ness that comes from God.

The closer we live in fellowship with Christ, the more conscious we shall be of how far short we fall of being what we ought to be for him. This consciousness, if kept alive in our lives, will be a major factor in moving us toward maturity in and for Christ. May he help each one of us to grow more and more in his likeness and increasingly may others see something of our resurrected Lord revealed in us.

> More like the Master I would live and grow;
>   More of His love to others I would show;
> More self-denial, like His in Galilee,
>   More like the Master I long to ever be.
> —CHARLES H. GABRIEL

# CHAPTER VI

# The Crucified Life

*From that time Jesus began to show his disciples that*
*he must go to Jerusalem and suffer many things from*
*the elders and chief priests and scribes, and be killed,*
*and on the third day be raised. . . .*
*Then Jesus told his disciples, "If any man would come*
*after me, let him deny himself and take up his cross*
*and follow me. For whoever would save his life will*
*lose it, and whoever loses his life for my sake will find*
*it.—Matthew 16:21,24–25*

Our preceding studies have all been based on passages from the epistles of Paul. We do not think this study of "Real Life in Christ" would be complete without some consideration of the crucifixion, its place in the life of Christ and in the lives of his disciples. The best passage for such a study is a portion of the marvelous conversation of Jesus with his disciples at Caesarea Philippi. So, for this study we turn from Paul to Jesus and to as challenging a statement as he ever made.

Let us begin with those three words in Matthew 16:21: "from that time." These words introduce a major phase of the public ministry of Jesus. Beginning with "from that time" in Matthew 4:17, Jesus had concentrated on the proclamation of the kingdom of heaven. Now, in the district or general area of Caesarea Philippi, about six to nine months before his crucifixion, he began to concentrate ("to speak plainly," TLB) on the place and meaning of the cross in his life and in the lives of his disciples. This represented a turning-point in his life, a watershed of the gospel. The stream began to flow with increasing rapidity toward Jerusalem and the cross.

What was the immediate background for the words "from that time"? What had happened that made this an appropriate time for him to begin to reveal more fully and plainly the kind of messiah he had come to be and the demands this placed on his followers? He had asked the disciples, "Who do men say that the Son of man is?" Possibly with different ones speaking up, they had answered, "Some say John the Baptist, others say Elijah, and others Jeremiah or one of the prophets." Then he asked them a very personal and a more important question, "But who do you say that I am?" Wouldn't we like to know the look out of his eyes and the tone of his voice as he asked the question? His eyes may have moved from face to face as he quietly asked the question in a tone that reached the depths of their souls. Typically, Peter answered, and I believe not just for himself but for all of them, "You are the Christ, the Son of the living God."

Peter and the other apostles had been closely associated with Jesus for approximately two and a half years. They had walked the dusty roads and trails with him. They had eaten with him, had slept out under the stars with him. They had heard the marvelous words that fell from his lips. They had seen him perform outstanding miracles. They had sensed his concern for people, for all kinds of people. They had heard him talk to God and talk to people about God. They did not understand fully, particularly the kind of messiah he had come to be, but they had at least come to the tentative conclusion that he was the promised Messiah, the anointed of God.

## The Cross of Christ

The fact that the disciples did not comprehend the place of the cross in the life of Jesus is evident in the sudden and strong reaction of Peter when Jesus revealed to them that he was going to Jerusalem to die. Possibly drawing Jesus aside, Peter said, "God forbid, Lord! This shall never happen to you": the "never" is the strongest possible way to express the negative. Peter's reaction was representative of the typical Jewish perspective concerning the Messiah. They expected him to triumph completely. Crucifixion on a cross for them would mean defeat.

Jesus reacted promptly and strongly to Peter's protest. It is possible that Jesus broke in and did not permit him to complete his statement ("and Peter . . . began to rebuke"). Possibly turning his back on Peter, Jesus said to him, "Get behind me, Satan!" Jesus saw in the words of Peter a renewal of the temptation of Satan to take the way of power rather than the way of the cross.

We should not be too hard on Peter. From this side of the cross we may see that the cross was necessary. But most of us are quite limited in our understanding of that cross. What do we visualize when we think of the word "cross"? Doubtlessly most of us see a cross on a hill outside the wall of Jerusalem. Or, we may see three crosses with the central one more prominent than the others. In other words, we tend to identify "the cross" entirely with the death of Christ. That was a very real cross on which he died. But the cross also represents a way of life. He lived the crosslike life. He gave himself unselfishly to the fulfillment of the will of God and in service to mankind. His death on the cross was a more or less natural extension or culmination of the kind of life he had lived.

Entirely too many of us would restrict the cross to Christ. We sing of the old rugged cross "on a hill far away" and that is where many of us want it to stay. As John Bright once said, "We want no part of it. We are possessed of the notion that the cross is for Christ, a once-and-for-all thing of the past tense." The cross, however, has a place in our lives and belongs in every tense: past, present, future.

The more serious we become as Christians the more clearly we will see that the cross is not to be restricted to Christ.

> Must Jesus bear the cross alone,
>> And all the world go free?
> No, there's a cross for every one,
>> And there's a cross for me.

## Its Meaning

Jesus not only wanted his disciples to understand that he had to go to Jerusalem and suffer many things from the elders, chief priests, and scribes (the three groups in the Sanhedrin), be put to death and on the third day be raised. He also wanted them to understand that if they wanted to go with him they were (1) to deny self, (2) take up their cross, and (3) follow him.

Notice "come after me" and "follow me." He never asks a disciple of his to go before him, the disciple is to follow his Master or Teacher. We can be assured that our Master has already walked in the way he asks us to walk. He is the full and perfect example of all he asks us to do and to be. He blazes many a trail for his disciples, trails at times that only he could blaze.

Now, what did Jesus mean when he said that the disciple should take up his cross? The idea of taking up a cross was familiar to the disciples. They knew that the condemned man had to carry the cross on which he was to be crucified to the place of crucifixion. But they were not going to Jerusalem to be crucified with him. What did he mean by their cross?

There are some mistaken ideas that are more or less prevalent. Jesus was certainly not referring to any physical cross, whether it be a cross around the neck or on the lapel of a coat or a literal cross of wood. Neither can the taking up of a cross be equated with some material sacrifice for the sake of others or for the cause of Christ. "Denying self is not to be confused with denying something to oneself" (*Broadman*). Possibly the most common mistaken idea is that the cross refers to some suffering or burden that has come upon one. How often have you heard someone say in the time of personal sorrow or suffering, "I guess this is my cross, I will have to bear it"?

The "cross" entails suffering but all suffering cannot be equated with the cross. It must be suffering that is voluntary and redemptive. The suffering that comes into our lives through the operation of the laws of life may be reacted to in such a way as to have a redemptive influence. Insofar as this is true, such suffering may be properly considered expressive of the crosslike life.

As previously implied, a part of the answer to the meaning of the cross is seen in the statement by Jesus. To deny self is to take up a cross. It means "yes to God and no to self." In other words, to take up a cross means to live for others and for God rather than for yourself.

How can we best summarize what it means for a Christian to take up a cross? A cross is something on which one is crucified. Hence, to take up a cross means to crucify self with selfish ambitions and purposes. Paul, particularly in Galatians, gives us considerable insight into the meaning of the cross in the Christian's life. For example, he said, "Those who belong to Christ Jesus have crucified ("put to death," TEV) the flesh ("their human nature," TEV; "the lower nature," NEB) with its passions and desires" (Gal. 5:24). Again Paul said, "Far be it from me to glory except in the cross of our Lord Jesus Christ, by which the world has been crucified to me, and I to the world" (Gal. 6:14). In Romans Paul said, "We know that our old self ("the men we once were," NEB) was crucified with him so that the sinful body might be destroyed, and we might no longer be enslaved to sin" (Rom. 6:6). Notice the things that Paul said had been crucified to or for him: the flesh or human or lower nature, the world, and his old self or "the man he once was."

The nearest thing to a definition of the Christian's cross or what it means to be crucified is Paul's statement: "I have been crucified with Christ; it is no longer I who live, but Christ who lives in me; and the life

I now live in the flesh I live by faith in the Son of God, who loved me and gave himself for me" (Gal. 2:20). In the expression "the life I now live" the emphasis is on "now." Paul drew a sharp contrast between his life in the past and the life he had lived since he had been crucified with Christ. Formerly, the "I" was central, now "Christ" was at the center. It is glorious to remember, however, that resurrection follows crucifixion. This is just as true in the life of the child of God as it was in the life of Christ. Paul had been crucified with Christ. Just as surely he had been raised with him. He walked in union with Christ. He could say, "For to me to live is Christ" (Phil. 1:21). We cannot truthfully say the same, but this should be the goal of our lives.

### Its Nature

An examination of Matthew 16:24, along with the parallel passages in Mark (8:34) and Luke (9:23) suggest several things concerning the nature of the Christian's cross-bearing or crucifixion.

1. *It is voluntary.* Notice "If any man ("anyone," NEB) would ("wants," TEV; or "wishes to," NEB) come after me." There is no outer compulsion. Jesus himself had an inner compulsion that was driving him toward Jerusalem and crucifixion. If one is to follow him, the motivation must come from within. Even the words "take up" imply a voluntary act. Jesus always left it to the free choice of men whether or not they followed him. He gave the invitation, "Follow me." They had to give the response. This is just as true today as it was when he walked among men. He has no draftees in his army. They must all be volunteers.

2. *It is necessary*. Jesus does not force one to take up a cross. On the other hand, one cannot follow him unless he denies himself and takes up his cross. Jesus was going to Jerusalem and the cross. If the disciples wanted to travel that road with him they had to deny themselves and take up their cross. On another occasion he had said, "And he who does not take his cross and follow me is not worthy of me" (Matt. 10:38). In even stronger language he once said, "Whoever does not bear his own cross and come after me ("follow in my footsteps," Phillips), cannot be my disciple" (Luke 14:27).

The cross for Jesus "was a necessity within freedom" (*Broadman*). If we are to follow him, we must take up our cross, but we are free to decide whether or not we will follow him.

Since none of us is perfect it seems necessary to say that to the degree we deny self and take up our cross to that degree only will we follow him. Or, the statement might be reversed: to the degree we follow him to that degree we will deny self or crucify self. We should never forget, however, what Bonhoeffer said, "When Christ calls a man he bids him come and die."

3. *It is personal*. "If any man" or "anyone" (NEB) applies to you, to me, to other men and women as individuals. No one can take up a cross for another: father for son, mother for daughter, pastor for people. Taking up a cross is an extremely personal matter.

4. *It is universal*. Here is where the other Synoptic Gospels help us. Combining Matthew, Mark, and Luke, the statement of Jesus would read as follows: "And he called to him the multitude with his disciples

(Mark 8:34), and said to all (Luke 9:23), 'If any man would come after me, let him deny himself and take up his cross and follow me.' '' In other words, this challenge was addressed not only to the inner circle of the twelve but to the multitude or to all.

To modernize the application: it is not just the missionary, the pastor, or someone else in a church-related vocation who is to deny self and take up his cross. No, the challenge applies to all of God's children, to those in the pew as well as in the pulpit. What a revolution would take place in our churches if all of us took seriously the challenge of Jesus to go with him to the cross!

5. *It is a continuing challenge*. We cannot take up a cross or crucify self once for all. Luke says "take up his cross daily." Williams translates Matthew 16:24 as follows: "If anyone wants to be my disciple, he must say 'No' to self, put his cross on his shoulders, and keep on following me." Notice the "keep on following me," which expresses continuous action. To "keep on following" him we must keep on denying or saying No to self—must keep on taking up our cross. It is a day-by-day experience.

### Its Results

What will be the results of our denying self and taking up our cross? Or, what will happen if we crucify self? There are at least three wonderful results, one of which was specifically stated by Jesus at Caesarea Philippi.

1. *We will find life*. It is a fundamental law of life that resurrection follows crucifixion. This was true in the life of Jesus. He never mentioned his death on the cross without at the same time mentioning his resur-

rection. He predicted his resurrection to his enemies (Matt. 12:40; John 2:19–21). At Caesarea Philippi he specifically foretold his resurrection to his disciples, which he repeated on subsequent occasions (Matt. 17:23; 20:19; 26:32). This was an idea that was difficult for the disciples to comprehend. They had seen him raise others from the dead but who would raise him?

What was to be true of him, he said, would also be true of them. They would find life by losing life: in other words, resurrection would follow crucifixion. *The New English Bible* translates verse 25 as follows: "Whoever cares for his own safety is lost; but if a man will let himself be lost for my sake, he will find his true self." This, "one of the profoundest things of Christ . . . he repeated many times" (Robertson). It is found with some variations in all four Gospels (Matt. 10:39; 16:25; Mark 8:34; Luke 9:23; 14:27; John 12:25). These words of Jesus are not merely good advice to be taken or ignored. "They are unbreakable truth" (Interpreter's). They state *the* basic law of the universe, which is operative in every area of life: physical, social, as well as spiritual. If we had eyes to see we would see a cross at the center of God's universe. The first law of life is not self-preservation but self-denial or self-giving.

Let us restate the basic truth: we discover real or abundant life by losing life, we find our true self by denying or sacrificing self. Or, as stated previously, resurrection always follows crucifixion. It possibly should be added that it must be a real crucifixion. No "playlike" or "pretended" crucifixion will be followed by resurrection. Also, it must be a crucifixion for his (Christ's) sake. Only those who have so crucified self can ever know the abundant or full life that is possible for them in Christ. In other words, the child of God must empty himself if he is to be filled from above.

2. *We shall give life to others*. We not only find life by losing life, we also give life by losing life. When his death on the cross was immediately ahead of him, Jesus said, "The hour has come for the Son of man to be glorified." There then follows God's basic law of life: "Truly, truly, I say unto you, unless a grain of wheat falls into the earth and dies, it remains alone, but if it dies, it bears much fruit" (John 12:23-24). This law which is operative in the physical world was applied by Jesus to the social and the spiritual realms. "The law of the seed is the law of human life" (Expositors'). In a statement similar to Matthew 16:25 he said, "He who loves his life loses it, and he who hates his life in this world will keep it for eternal life" or, as Williams, correctly suggesting that there are two different words for life in the statement, translates it, "Whoever loves his lower life will lose the higher; but whoever hates his lower life in this world preserves the higher for eternal life" (John 12:25). Jesus also applied the law of the seed to the redemption of mankind. He said, " 'And I, when I am lifted up from the earth will draw all men to myself.' He said this to show by what death he was to die" (vv. 32-33).

Again, we can say that to the degree we deny self and take up our cross to that degree only will we be a redeeming influence among men. Fruit, in the spiritual as well as in the natural order, is the result of a death.

3. *We will reveal Christ*. Do you remember the words of Jesus to a small group of his disciples on

the occasion of one of his resurrection appearances? His statement to them was, "As the Father has sent me, even so I send you" (John 20:21). I never will forget when that statement really gripped my life several years ago. There are few verses with a greater challenge. I am persuaded that Christ would present this same challenge to us today.

From the time these words gripped me I have been asking and seeking to answer some questions. What did Jesus mean when he said, "As the Father has sent me, even so I send you"? Let me suggest two or three things that I think he must have meant. He had a deep sense of having been sent. The word "send" or "sent" was a frequently used word by Jesus. It is one of the key words in John's gospel. This sense of having been sent gave him a sense of holy urgency. He must work the works of him that sent him while it was day, the night would come when no man could work. Jesus had a sense of having been sent to redeem man and to reveal God. These two purposes were so closely interrelated that it is difficult to determine which one was primary. The main thing from our perspective is that to reveal God and particularly God's attitude toward man and to redeem man Christ had to go to the cross. In other words, his crucifixion was necessary if he was to accomplish the purposes of the Father.

To sum up, his words could mean: "Just as the Father sent me, so send I you. He sent me to do his will, you are sent to do my will. He sent me to redeem man, you are sent to be a redeeming influence among men. He sent me to reveal him, you are sent to reveal me and hence to reveal him."

Christ was God incarnate or God in human flesh. We are to be Christ incarnate, the only revelation of Christ many people will ever see. The great Japanese Christian, Kagawa, once said that each Christian is a little Christ. What kind of a conception of Christ do people get when they look at our lives? That will be determined by how completely and consistently we follow him, which in turn will be determined to a large degree by how thoroughly we deny self and take up our cross. In other words, the impact we make on others for Christ will be determined by how fully we walk in his way instead of in our own way. His way of obedience led him to Jerusalem and the cross. If we walk in his way it will take us to our Jerusalem and our cross.

## Conclusion

From Caesarea Philippi to his death in Jerusalem the cross was a continuing topic of conversation by Jesus. The next recorded incident in his life was the experience on the Mount of Transfiguration. Luke gives us the topic of conversation: "Two men talked with him, Moses and Elijah, who appeared in glory and spoke of his departure ("decease," KJV), which he was to accomplish at Jerusalem" (Luke 9:30–31). Between Caesarea Philippi and the transfiguration was "the silent week" What do you suppose Jesus did during that week? Does it not seem natural to believe that one main thing he did was to attempt to help his disciples to understand the significance of the cross in his life and in their lives?

A few months after Caesarea Philippi there came the "garden" experience. What was central in that experience? It was a struggle regarding the will of God. To accept the Father's will meant the crucifixion. There was acceptance of or cooperation with the will of God from the first. The prayer of Jesus was, "My Father, if it be possible, let this cup pass from me." What cup? There are several things it could refer to but will you not agree that supremely the cup referred to his suffering on the cross, suffering that was not exclusively physical? Then came from his lips those matchless words, "nevertheless, not as I will, but as thou wilt" (Matt. 26:39). Here was the inner crucifixion that preceded the literal physical crucifixion.

There followed Calvary but also, thank the Lord, the empty tomb. Let us repeat the wonderful truth that resurrection always follows a real crucifixion. (Our next study will be on "The Resurrected Life.") We find life by losing it.

I am sure I have been influenced more than most by an occasional incidental statement that was dropped into my life. One such statement was made by a missionary in a chapel service several years ago. He told something about what he and his family gave up to go to the mission field. He than told of individuals who had been brought to the Lord and churches they had founded. Theirs had been a rich and full life in the work of the Lord. Then he made the statement that has stayed with me through the years and has become a part of my basic philosophy of life. His statement was: "The Lord has so ordered things that we cannot make a real sacrifice for him." When we feel that we have paid a price for following him and his will, he repays us so abundantly that we see we have not made any real sacrifice.

It pays to serve Jesus,
  It pays every day,
It pays every step of the way.

It costs but it also pays rich dividends to follow him.

# CHAPTER VII

# The Resurrected Life

*If then you have been raised with Christ . . . seek
the things that are above. . . . Put to death,
. . . what is earthly in you. . . . Put on then as
God's chosen ones . . . and above all of these put
on love.*—Colossians 3:1–14

It is logical to follow a study of "The Crucified Life"
with one on "The Resurrected Life." The final word
of God is never "death" but "life," although it may
be life through death.

Need I remind you that in these studies together
we are concerned primarily with everyday Christian
living? This passage from Colossians stands at the
beginning of the more practical portion of the epistle.
"Paul turns from expounding the fulness of Christ
. . . to describing the fulness of the Christian life"
(Broadman). The word "therefore" may not be
found in the translations but the therefore perspective
is present. Really "then" could be "therefore": it is
the same word (*oun*) translated "therefore" in Romans
12:1, Ephesians 4:1, and many other places.

The "if" is not of conjecture but of assumption or
"logical sequence." Moffatt and *The Living Bible*
say "since," while *Today's English Version* makes

the first portion of the verse a simple statement of fact: "You have been raised with Christ." When had they been raised with Christ? Ideally in his resurrection, actually or biographically when they were brought into union with the resurrected Christ.

Paul here was tying on to and developing something he had said previously: "You were buried with him in baptism, in which you were also raised with him from the dead" (Col. 2:12). Here in 3:1 Paul used the baptismal imagery but he referred to something deeper, which baptism symbolizes but which also gives baptism its greatest significance. It may be stated as follows: our union with Christ brings us into the resurrected state; he has been raised; we have been raised with him. This is another of the great blessings we have in Christ, and "Real Life in Christ" is the general theme of this series of messages.

What kind of a life should one live who has been raised with Christ? Some things are suggested by Paul that will search our souls if we will let them.

### Its Eternal Aspects (vv. 1–4)

Paul first suggested to the Colossians and would suggest to us that since we have been raised with Christ, we should seek or set our minds on things above. As usual, Williams brings out the verb tense: "keep on seeking," "practice occupying your mind." One who has been raised with Christ should "keep on seeking" things above "as the exile seeks home." We are "strangers here within a foreign land."

Pascal suggests that we could not seek God unless we in some sense, and I would add "to some degree," already possessed him. We seek the things above because the One who lives above also lives within us. We have had at least a glimpse of things eternal. The clearer the glimpse the greater the desire for a fuller vision of the eternal. This is a major factor in the restlessness of the serious Christian.

Possibly it should be added that there is nothing inherently evil in the material and the earthly. It is not money or the things that money can buy that are evil. It is "the love of money [that] is the root of all evil" (1 Tim. 6:10). Material things, things that are transient or passing, should never be first in the life of one who has been raised with Christ. It was Jesus who said that his disciples should not treasure the treasures of earth. They cannot serve God and mammon. They should seek first the kingdom of God and trust their heavenly Father to provide for them the necessities of life (Matt. 6:19–34). Things on the earth become sinful "if sought and thought on in preference to things above" (*Expositors'*).

Paul, in this passage from Colossians, suggests at least three reasons or motives for seeking things above:

(1) Christ with whom we have been raised is there "seated on the right hand of God," "in the place of honor and power" (TLB).

(2) We died and our life is hid with Christ in God. Notice the verb tenses: "we died" and "our life is hid." "The 'death' is fact accomplished, the resulting 'life' is fact continuing" (*Cambridge*). This is one of the marvelous paradoxes of the Scriptures: we have died yet we live. Really, we live with him because we have died with him. As we said in our last study together, there is no death with and in him without a resurrection.

We should seek things above because we are hid with Christ in God. Hid in the sense that this new life is a mystery. We cannot fully understand it. It is beyond our comprehension. In addition to the mystery of our relation to him we are also hid in the sense of concealment and security or safety. What a glorious truth. You remember the great statement by Jesus. He said that he gave his sheep eternal life and that "no one shall snatch them out of my hand . . . no one is able to snatch them out of the Father's hand. I and the Father are one" (John 10:28–30). We are in his hand. His hand is in the Father's hand. What security!

(3) Another reason or motive for seeking things above or things eternal is the fact that Christ will appear or be manifested and we with him. As surely as we are hid with him now, we will appear or be manifested with him when he comes again. It is then that "the verdicts of eternity will reverse the verdicts of time" (Barclay).

Notice the change of pronouns from "your life" in verse 3 to "our life" in verse 4. In the latter Paul seemed to hasten to include himself. What did he mean when he said, "Christ who is our life"? He did not say, "Christ who gives us life" but "who *is* our life." *Today's English Version* says, "Your real life is in Christ." "Real life" for the child of God is the product of his union with Christ. John said, "He who has the Son has life" (1 John 5:12). Paul said, "For to me to live is Christ" (Phil. 1:21) or "For what is life? to me, it is Christ" (TEV).

## Its Negative Aspects (vv. 5–9)

The resurrection life not only has its eternal aspects; it also has some negative aspects. There are some things that do not belong in the life of one who has been raised with Christ. They are out of harmony with that life.

The emphasis on the negatives begins with a general exhortation: "Put to death therefore what is earthly in you." The mortifying (KJV) or putting to death carries the idea of a single decisive act: "So once for all put to death your lower earthly nature" (Williams). The "therefore" could refer to that which immediately precedes it: "You also will appear with him in glory." But it could also go back to verse 1: "Since you have been raised with Christ." These words could properly serve as an introduction to verse 5: "Since you have been raised with Christ, put to death therefore what is earthly in you."

It has been suggested that Paul compressed his negative exhortations into two pentads (vv. 5 and 8) and his positive instruction into one pentad (v. 12). (A pentad is a series or group of five.) In other words, there are two lists of vices and one of virtues. An examination of the two lists of vices will reveal three major and familiar types of sins.

(1) *Sins of the flesh*: immorality or "fornication" (KJV) and impurity or "indecency" (TEV) —a broader concept than immorality or fornication, includes word and thought as well as deed.

(2) *Sins of the spoken word*: slander, "insults" (TEV), or "cursing" (NEB) and foul talk, "obscene

talk" (TEV), "filthy talk" (NEB), or abusive talk or language (*International*).

(3) *Sins of thought*: passion or "lust" (TEV), evil desire or evil passion—the word "evil" is used because passion or desire may be good, covetousness or "ruthless greed" (NEB) —"implies desire to have more than one's share of everything" (Moffatt), anger and wrath which might be considered sins of the tongue because they are usually expressed.

These things had once characterized their lives but now they are new creatures in Christ Jesus, they have been raised with him and are to live a different type and quality of life. These vices were incompatible with their new nature. This is seen in the special exhortation for them to stop lying to one another. The appeal or motive is: "seeing that you have put off the old nature with its practices" (v. 9).

Now, where do you and I have the greatest problem? I am sure that some of us feel the pressure of the temptations of the flesh. It will be wise for all of us to take heed lest we fall. Many men and women, highly respected for years of exemplary Christian behavior, seem to go to pieces morally and fall into the grossest sins.

But I assume that more of us have a problem with our tongues, with the spoken word. We may be tempted to be harshly or unfairly critical or to pass on gossip. Or, we may have a weakness regarding swearing or cursing. Or, we may have a tendency to tell dirty or shady stories. There are few things that I have detested any more through the years than a dirty story. I would rather a man would plainly "cuss" in my presence than to tell a filthy story. I am sure one reason for this is the fact that I heard so many such stories where I worked when I was a youngster. Some of those I still wish I could erase from my mind.

I have heard on more than one occasion a story regarding B. H. Carroll, a physical and spiritual giant in the Southwest some years ago. He was in the presence of a group of men. One man glanced around and said, "I see there are no ladies in the crowd" and started to tell an off-color story. B. H. Carroll stood straight and tall, all six feet four inches of him, and said, "There may not be any ladies present but there is at least one gentleman" and left the group.

Am I correct when I suggest that most of us have the greatest problem with the sins of the mind, the mediations of the heart? We should remember that Jesus made sin inner as well as outer: "I say to you that every one who looks at a woman lustfully has already committed adultery with her in his heart" (Matt. 5:28). The fact that sin can be inner should give to each of us a deepened sense of sin in our lives. We need to remember also that what is within tends sooner or later to be expressed outwardly. Will you not agree that we could wisely pray every day:

> Let the words of my mouth and the
>  meditations of my heart
> be acceptable in thy sight,
> O Lord, my rock and my redeemer.
>  (Ps. 19:14)

### Its Positive Aspects (vv. 10–14)

Paul was a realist. He believed that union with Christ or being raised with Christ meant a new kind of life. But he was also convinced that the initial experience in and with the resurrected Christ "was no prescription for instant holiness" (Broadman). Notice what he said in verse 10. The Colossians had put on the new nature or "a brand new kind of life" (TLB). But the new nature or new kind of life which had been put on was "being renewed in knowledge after the image of its creator." The "new" was "being renewed." The new nature is dynamic, not static. It is both a present reality and a future hope, an achievement but also a process. Paul speaks of "death to the old and life to the new either as ideally complete in the moment of conversion or realized gradually in actual experience" (Expositors').

The conviction of Paul that the child of God was a new man in need of constant renewal helps to explain the considerable attention he gives in his epistles to instruction in everyday Christian living. Here in Colossians 3 as elsewhere he begins with negative instruction, followed by the positive.

In verse 11 Paul says that "here," in this new relation or new nature, there is no room for human distinctions that divide. The distinctions or differences listed represent major classifications that separate: racial differences—Greek and Jew; religious differences—circumcised and uncircumcised; cultural differences—barbarian, Scythian; social differences—slave, free man. Through the restoration of the image of God which results from being raised with Christ "the fundamental unity of the human race is restored" (Interpreter's). Notice the closing words of verse 11: "but Christ is all, and in all." All human differences that divide merge in him. "Christ has obliterated the words barbarian, master, slave, all of them and has substituted the word *adelphos* (brother)'' (Robertson).

If Paul were writing to us or to one of our churches today he would doubtlessly use contemporary differences but he would make the same general emphasis. What do you think might be some of the differences he would mention: black and white? educated and uneducated? rich and poor? American and Russian? It seems to me that Paul implied that to the degree we have matured in our relation to the resurrected Christ, to the degree that the image of God has been restored in us to that degree we will be free from the divisive distinctions characteristic of our contemporary society. What do you think?

Beginning with verse 12 there is stated in a specific way some of the positive aspects or characteristics of the resurrected life. Again let us insert the first words of verse 1: "Since you have been raised with Christ, put on then . . . " Here Paul used the figure of changing a garment. They have been exhorted to put off the old; now he exhorts them to put on the new. He spoke of them as "God's chosen ones, holy and beloved." In the Old Testament Israel was God's chosen people, holy or dedicated, and beloved. Now, those who have come into the spiritual family of God through their union with Christ are the chosen ones.

Next, let us notice the positive qualities that Paul mentioned. Except for the first two they are the same ones mentioned in Ephesians 4:2. This should not surprise us since Ephesians and Colossians are very closely related. There are few passages of Scripture that search my soul more than verses 12–14 of this chapter from Colossians. Will you read them quietly and prayerfully? Notice that all of these virtues are in the area of man-to-man or human relationships.

The qualities are *compassion*, *kindness*—"the character which offers sympathy and invites confidence" (*Cambridge*) or as Trench says, "a lovely word for a lovely quality," lowliness ("*humility*," TEV), meekness ("*gentleness*," TEV), and *patience* ("longsuffering," KJV). I have been a teacher most of my life. It is natural for me to think in terms of grading. If you graded yourself by letter grades, A, B, C, D, F, how would you grade regarding compassion and kindness? What about humility, gentleness, and patience? On which one would you grade highest? On which lowest? Would you grade F on one or more of these virtues? The questions I have asked you I have asked myself many times.

Just as he did regarding the negatives, Paul gave special emphasis to a closing positive exhortation: forbearance and forgiveness (cf. Eph. 4:2—"forbearing one another in love"). Notice here that Paul did not say, "Forgive others" but rather "forgive each other." The need for mutual forbearance and forgiveness was assumed.

Also notice that Paul said that we should forgive one another "as the Lord" has forgiven us. Here the *forgiveness* of the Lord is not example. Rather, the motive for our forgiving one another is the fact that he has forgiven us: "as the Lord has forgiven you." And he has had to forgive much more in us than we will ever have to forgive in another. The forgiven sinner should be the forgiving sinner. We know by what Jesus said in and regarding the model prayer that it is also true that the forgiving sinner will be the forgiven sinner:

"For if you forgive men their trespasses, your heavenly Father also will forgive you: but if you do not forgive men their trespasses, neither will your Father forgive your trespasses" (Matt. 6:14–15).

"Above all these" qualities, the Colossians were admonished to "*put on love*, which binds everything together in perfect harmony" ("unity," TEV). There are two interpretations of "above all these." One is the suggestion that it simply means "in addition to all these" or "and to all these add love" (Phillips). The other viewpoint, which seems preferable to me, is that Paul was using here as previously the figure of clothing. As Lightfoot and others suggest, those who have been raised with Christ are to put on love as an outer garment or girdle that will hold all the other garments or virtues in place. Love is "the crown of all the Christian virtues" (*Interpreter's*). It "embraces and knits together all the virtues" (Vincent) or it "binds the virtues into a harmonious whole" (*International*). Phillips, in his typically interpretative translation, says, "Love is the golden chain of all the virtues."

Love is not only the bond that binds all the virtues into a harmonious whole in our individual lives; it is also the bond that binds Christians together in unity or the secret to harmony in the Christian fellowship.

## Conclusion

We have suggested that since we have been raised with Christ (1) we should seek or set our minds on things above, (2) we should put out of our lives anything that is out of harmony with living the resurrected life, and (3) we should put on or build into our lives those qualities that should naturally evolve from our union with Christ. It has also been stated that through our resurrection with Christ we have become new men and women. However, this renewal, and hence our resurrection, is not only a present reality but also a future hope.

As we mature in our relations to and with the resurrected Christ the negatives of the Christian life will be of decreasing importance. In contrast, the positives will be accentuated increasingly. The supreme test of our resurrected state is how much we have become like the One with whom we have been raised.

Many times when I have thought about being raised with Christ, my mind has turned to Lazarus. What do you suppose was the effect on Lazarus of the fact that Jesus brought him forth from the grave? We do know that "Lazarus was one of those at table with him" (John 12:2) when some friends had a supper for Jesus a short time before his crucifixion. It would be natural for Lazarus to want to be with Jesus as much as possible. Also, I am persuaded that Lazarus wanted to do only those things that he thought would be approved by the One who had raised him from the dead.

If these things were true of Lazarus who had been raised from physical death, should they not be just as true of you and me who have been raised from spiritual death to walk in newness of life with our risen Lord? Do we have a deep desire to walk in the consciousness of his presence? Do we have an abiding purpose to do only the things that will please him?

# CHAPTER VIII

# The Peaceful Life

*Peace I leave with you; my peace I give to you; not as the world gives do I give to you. Let not your hearts be troubled, neither let them be afraid*—John 14:27
*I have said this to you, that in me you may have peace. In the world you have tribulation; but be of good cheer, I have overcome the world.*—John 16:33

The preceding discussions have majored on the challenge contained in "Real Life in Christ." This, the closing discussion, will contain an element of challenge but it will be primarily a message of encouragement and comfort. I personally do not think our study of "Real Life in Christ" would be complete without some consideration of the peace that passes understanding which can and should come into our lives as a result of our being in Christ and he in us.

This discussion of peace will not be as largely exegetical or expository as most of the preceding chapters. Rather, the emphasis will be on the study of an idea (peace) but with some particular attention to two verses from John's Gospel. These verses come from the conversations of Jesus with his disciples immediately preceding his arrest, trial, crucifixion, and resurrection. The conversations are found only in John's Gospel.

How grateful we should be for the four Gospels, which frequently supplement one another in striking and significant ways.

Notice in 16:33 that Jesus said, "I have said this to you" or "These things I have spoken unto you" (KJV). To what does "this" or "these things" refer? It is possible that the reference is simply to the preceding verse: the disciples would be scattered but they should remember that he would not be alone "for the Father" would be with him. But there is also a possibility that "this" or "these things" refer to all he had said as recorded in chapters 14, 15, and 16, opening with the words " 'Let not your hearts be troubled' " (14:1). In these conversations Jesus had spoken to them words of consolation and comfort. These things he had said that they might "keep having peace" (Robertson). They could "keep having peace" even when he was put to death.

### Its Meaning

As is true of many words, "peace" is used with different meanings or emphases. In the Scriptures there are three major ways in which the word is used. At times these tend to blend into one another.

Peace or *shalom*, the Hebrew word, was the ordinary Oriental greeting or farewell. Jesus on some occasions used "peace" in this way. For example, when he appeared to his disciples after his resurrection his initial word to them was, "Peace be with you" (John 20:19,21,26). Paul used "peace," along with "grace," in the salutation of all his epistles, with the addition of "mercy" in his letters to Timothy. In practically all cases it was the grace and peace "from God our

Father and the Lord Jesus Christ." One epistle (Romans) closes, except for a chapter of personalized greetings, with "The God of peace be with you" (Rom. 15:33). While the preceding suggests that Paul used "peace" as a form of greeting or farewell, it was more than a mere formality. It was peace from God who was a God of peace.

"Peace" is also used in the Scriptures to refer to human peace. This might be peace between individuals, peace among nations, or peace in the world in general. Jesus suggested that men should be "at peace with one another" (Mark 9:50). Paul admonished the Thessalonians: "Be at peace among yourselves" (1 Thess. 5:13). To the Corinthians he said, "God has called us to peace" (1 Cor. 7:15). He also admonished them to "live in peace" and added the promise, "and the God of love and peace will be with you" (2 Cor. 13:11). To the Romans he suggested, "If possible so far as it depends upon you, live peaceably with all" (Rom. 12:18). Also to the Romans he said, "Let us then pursue what makes for peace and for mutual upbuilding" (14:19). The writer of Hebrews admonished, "Strive for peace with all men" (Heb. 12:14). Peter said that all those to whom he wrote should "seek peace and pursue it" (1 Pet. 3:11); they should "be zealous to be . . . at peace" (2 Pet. 3:14). It is evident from the context that this meant peace with one another.

Possibly it should be added that peace for the Christian, as is true of love, looks in two directions. It looks to God who through Christ gives us peace. In turn, the peace we have from and with God will motivate or lead us to live at peace with one another. The latter, peace with our fellowman, is both a product and an evidence of our peace with God.

Jesus took common words and transformed them. He breathed new life and depth into them. This was true of his use of "peace." As suggested previously, he used the word in its usual sense of greeting or farewell. He also referred to human peace. But he also spoke of an inner spiritual peace, of peace with God and of a consequent peace from God, which can become the inner possession of the child of God. Such peace was and is a gift from God but for it to become a reality it must also, like other gifts of God, be an achievement.

It is this inner spiritual peace to which Jesus referred in John 14:27 and 16:33. The close proximity of "peace" and "fear" in 14:27 suggests that "peace" is the opposite of "fear." The latter implies that peace and faith are closely related. If our faith in the sovereign God of the universe is strong and stable we will not be afraid, we will have peace within. The peaceful heart is quiet and calm in the face of life and its problems. It has learned to rest in the Lord, to trust his presence and promises. Such peace is not escape from the storms of life but a confident facing of the storms. Prior to the peace that comes from God is our peace with God. This peace is the product of faith: "Since we are justified by faith, we have peace with God through our Lord Jesus Christ" (Rom. 5:1).

An evangelist preaching on peace said that a storm was approaching. A submarine in the harbor went down and surfaced again after the storm was over. That was his illustration of peace. That is not Christian peace. A better illustration would be the giant ocean-going liner that rode out the storm. The Christian cannot escape the storms of life. He can, through the grace and strength that God gives, have peace in the midst of the storms. We should never forget that such peace is "the peace of God" (Col. 3:15) or "the peace that Christ gives" (TEV). The closing exhortation of Paul to the Thessalonians would be appropriate for us today: "Now may the Lord of peace himself give you peace at all times in all ways" (2 Thess. 3:16).

### Its Need

The disciples to whom Jesus spoke needed his encouraging words concerning peace. In a few short hours their Master and Leader would be arrested, tried, condemned to die, and crucified. He had spoken to them of his resurrection but they did not fully comprehend it. They desperately needed the words of Jesus, "Peace I leave with you; my peace I give to you."

Will you not agree that we also need the peace that he alone can give? There are so many things that tend to disturb us and rob us of the inner peace we should have. Sometimes the things that disturb us most are primarily selfish. These are the negative, self-defeating, destructive pressures and tensions. These are usually the result of too much self-centeredness and too little faith.

There are, however, some personal matters that should concern us. Most of us are disturbed, to varying degrees, because of the sins and failures in our lives. Have you ever in the quietness of your own home said to yourself, "I would hate for people to know me as I really am. I would hate for them to know my faults and failures, some of which God and I alone know about"? The tension this creates becomes much greater if we do not repent of our sins and failures and if after repentance we fail to appropriate the forgiveness of our heavenly Father. He is not only willing but anxious to forgive us.

Then there are the sorrows and burdens that come to all, sooner or later, as a part of life. Some of these are strictly personal; others are, to some degree, vicarious as we enter into the sorrows and burdens of loved ones, friends, and others.

Mommy and I have been members of our church for many years. We are well acquainted with many and possibly most of our fellow church members. Many of them have had and have heavy burdens to carry and deep and abiding sorrows in their lives. As I have looked over the congregation or as I have contemplated their burdens and sorrows, the familiar cry of Isaiah has frequently come to my mind: "Comfort ye, comfort ye, my people, saith your God" (Isa. 40:1, KJV).

Furthermore, some of us may be deeply concerned about conditions in our churches, in our nation, and in the world. We love our church and our nation but there may be tendencies within both that make it difficult for us to have the inner peace that we feel we need.

Some of us also may be concerned and fearful about the future. It seems that the future will be drastically different from the present. We are not sure what will be the shape of things to come. Let me share a story with you.

A number of years ago I was very seriously ill, as sick as one can be and come back to live. After four weeks in the hospital I was taken home in an ambulance. Our younger son, then about four and a half, began to ask many questions about heaven. (I have always been glad it wasn't about the other place.) As parents know, a four-year-old can ask questions that a wise man cannot answer. Frequently his mother or I said, "Eugene, we do not know much about heaven: where it is or what the conditions will be when we get there. There is one thing we do know: we know that Jesus will be there and if he is there that will be enough." We do not know much about what our world will be like twenty-five, fifty, or a hundred years from now. There is one thing, however, that we do know. We know that God will still be on his throne watching o'er his own. That is enough. We can simply trust the future with him as well as the past and the present.

Possibly a parenthetical statement should be made. We should remember that peace is only one side of the Christian life. Tension as well as peace is a natural and necessary phase of the truly Christian life. Here I am referring to what I prefer to call "constructive tension."

I have frequently told young preachers that if they want to be nice and warm and comfortable in the ministry they had better not get serious about being a real Christian and about doing anything much concerning the world in which they live. "If you get serious about being a real Christian instead of a merely nominal Christian, you are going to realize right soon how far short you fall of being what you ought to be. You will be under constant pressure or tension. Also, if you get serious about doing anything to lift the world toward the purposes of God for the world you will quickly recognize that the world falls far short of being what it ought to be. Furthermore, you will realize that there is comparatively little you can do to lift that world toward God.'' But I also have suggested to them and would suggest to you that there is no progress in the Christian life without the constructive tension that results from seeking seriously to be a real Christian. In other words, unless we are possessed with a holy discontent we will make little progress in our lives and will do little to move others, our churches, and our world toward God.

However, there may be involved here one of the marvelous paradoxes of the Christian life. In the midst of the tensions and pressures of life we can have as a backdrop for that tension the peace that passes understanding. Many of God's best men and women have a terrific inner drive to do more for the Lord and particularly to be more what he would have them to be. Sometimes for them the peace that God alone can give is all that makes life livable. But thanks be to God, all of us can have that peace through faith in the sovereign God of the universe!

## Its Source

Let us examine a little more thoroughly the various approaches men have made in their search for peace in the midst of the pressures and tensions that life brings. Some seek peace by ignoring the problems of life. There are others who seek peace by withdrawing as far as possible from the world and its problems. The latter is one of the historic strategies regarding the relation of the Christian and the church to the world.

It is followed in the contemporary period, to varying degrees, by Mennonites and other sectarian groups. In this way they may avoid some of the pressures and problems of the world but they cannot get away from the more personal tensions that tend to destroy one's peace of mind. And after all most Christians do not believe that the Lord approves any effort to separate themselves physically from the world. They remember that their Lord and Master prayed: "I do not pray that thou shouldst take them out of the world, but that thou shouldst keep them from the evil one" (John 17:15).

If tension arises in our lives because we are conscious of our sins and failures, we can contribute to our peace of mind by doing what we can to remove the causes of the tension. But when we do our very best we fall far short. When we fall short we can have peace within if we will repent, ask our heavenly Father to forgive us, and then really believe that he forgives.

We should never forget, however, that real Christian peace is the peace that Christ alone can give. He does not counsel peace, he gives it. Notice he said to the disciples, "My peace I give to you." The "my" is emphatic. Just as he speaks elsewhere in John's Gospel of "my judgment" (5:30), "my commandments" (14:15); "my love" (15:10); and "my joy" or "the joy that is mine" (17:13), so he speaks of "my peace" or "the peace that is mine." One cannot give to others that which he himself does not possess.

Jesus had little to leave his disciples. Even his clothes would soon be divided among those who crucified him. Peace was one thing that could not be taken from him. It was one thing he could leave to his disciples if they would accept it. The peace that he had as he faced death, he would give to the disciples as they faced the uncertainities and perils of the days immediately ahead. What an inheritance! So it is with us: he offers us his peace but we must accept it. We accept his peace by accepting him and letting him come into our lives. As Paul said, "he is our peace" (Eph. 2:14). It is the peace of Christ that rules or arbitrates in our lives (Col. 3:15). This peace is the fruit of the Spirit (Gal. 5:22).

Jesus also said to his disciples, "not as the world gives do I give to you." What a contrast between what he gives and what the world gives! The world gives with the expectation or hope of receiving something in return. It gives to friends and tends to withhold from enemies. It gives that which costs it little or nothing. The world even pretends to give that which is not its to give. It says, "Peace, peace" when there is no peace. Also, the world's gifts are greatest and most valued when first received.

In contrast to the world, Christ gives
    to those who cannot give anything in return;
    to both friend and foe or enemy;
    that which cost him his life,
    that which is his to give—
    gifts that grow in power and value.

In John 16:33, Jesus plainly said, "In me you may have peace. In the world you have tribulation." The fact that the child of God is in Christ but at the same time in the world is one of the sources of the tensions he has. In the midst of the tribulations or troubles of the world, however, the Christian can have peace, the peace that comes from an awareness of the presence of the indwelling Christ.

This one who offers his peace to us has "overcome the world." The awareness that this is true is another source of peace for us. Notice the verb tense of the statement: "I have overcome the world" not "will overcome." The "I" is emphatic. It was possible for him to say, "I have overcome the world" at the very time when it looked like the world had overcome him. *The New English Bible* translates the statement as follows: "But courage! The victory is mine; I have conquered the world." One source of this victory and the consequent peace he had was the consciousness that he was not alone, the Father was with him (16:32). The Father and he could face anything with calm assurance. Likewise, the indwelling victorious Christ and the child of God can together face anything.

The word translated "overcome" or "conquered" is found only here in John's gospel but is rather frequent in the other Johannine writings. In 1 John it is said that our faith overcomes the world but it is faith in the One who himself has overcome the world: "For whatever is born of God overcomes the world; and this is the victory that overcomes the world, our faith. Who is it that overcomes the world but he who believes that Jesus is the Son of God" (1 John 5:4–5). He overcame the world; we can overcome the world in the strength he will provide. He had peace; we can have his peace or peace that comes from him in the midst of the perplexities and pressures of the world.

> Faith is the victory!
> Oh, glorious victory
> That overcomes the world.

The great promises found in the Scriptures provide another source of peace for us. In a sense they are not "another source"; they are ours because we are his and dwell "in him" and he in us. Apart from our relation to the resurrected Christ the promises would be meaningless.

What are some of your favorite promises? It would be interesting and inspiring if we could exchange some of our favorites and give some experience in relation to them. Let me share with you a few of my favorites. You remember that the psalmist said, "Fret not thyself because of evildoers" (Ps. 37:1, KJV). In succeeding verses the psalmist gives the secret to the nonfretful or peaceful heart: "Trust in the Lord" (v. 3); "Delight thyself also in the Lord" (v. 4); "Commit thy way unto the Lord" (v. 5); and "Rest in the Lord, and wait patiently for him" (v. 7). These are all closely related. If these things characterize our lives, we can and will have the peace that comes from a consciousness of his presence.

When I think of one resting in the Lord, I visualize a person stretched out on a bed flat on his back, with his feet apart a few inches and with arms down at his sides. If he has learned the art of relaxation, and it is an art, he can feel his body relaxing and letting go, trusting the bed to hold him up. This is what happens when one "rests in the Lord." He lets go, he relaxes in the Lord. He can let go with the assurance that "underneath are the everlasting arms" (Deut. 33:27). These words come to my mind most frequently when I am about thirty to forty thousand feet in the air in a giant jet plane. I may be on one sometime that will go down, but even if that should happen, still underneath will be the everlasting arms.

These everlasting arms belong to the sovereign God

of the universe, and that sovereign God is our heavenly Father. He is also our shepherd and the shepherd knows his sheep by name. He makes us to lie down in green pastures, he leads us beside still waters or "the waters of gentle stillness."

There are many other wonderful promises that God will use, if we will let him, to give us quietness and peace in the midst of conditions in the world that tend to disturb us. One is the word of God to Paul, "My grace is sufficient for you" (2 Cor. 12:9). His grace will be sufficient for us whatever the situation may be. Have you ever felt that you were "at the end of your rope," when you felt that you could not go on? Have you at such a time asked the Lord to supply the strength and grace that was needed and felt new strength come into your life?

There have been times when I do not know what I would have done without Romans 8:28: "We know that in everything God works for good with those who love him, who are called according to his purpose." I like the Revised Standard translation of this verse better than the more familiar King James. Everything does not automatically work for good. No, God is the one who makes it possible for things to work together for good.

Permit me to mention one additional promise that has meant a great deal to me personally. I doubt if many of you will know that this one is in the Bible. I discovered it several years ago. I was about as despondent and blue that day as I ever get. I had an experience that I am sure many of you have had. I had occasion to read the book of Micah as I prepared a writing assignment. As I was reading, one verse seemed to jump out of the page at me. It provided a message that I desperately needed that day and have needed many times since. The words of the prophet were:

> When I fall, I shall rise;
> When I sit in darkness,
>     the Lord will be a light to me.
>
> (Mic. 7:8)

I was sitting in darkness that day. I found then and have discovered often since that day that if I will look to "the true Light, which lighteth every man that cometh into the world" (John 1:9, KJV), that that Light will dispel the darkness and restore to me the quietness and peace that I need.

## Its Results

What will be the results in our lives of this peace that Christ offers to us? Let us consider very briefly a couple of contributions it will make to our lives. If peace is consistently a part of the pattern of our lives *it will give us a depth and dignity* that otherwise will be lacking. You as I have seen a few real saints of God. I have seen them in various parts of the world; they are not restricted to any class or color. These saints, who have some of the glory of the Lord etched into their faces, have learned the art of resting in the Lord. The glory and the peace that are theirs are not determined by or dependent upon outer conditions. In the Lord they have overcome the world and the things of the world that would rob them of the peace of God.

Being able to rest in the Lord and to have the consequent peace of mind and heart *will enable us to do more for the Lord and our fellowman*. I have a doctor friend to whom I have been going for an annual physical check-up for many years. After he explains to me the results of the laboratory tests, the X-rays, and the examination in general, he usually writes out some instructions. In recent years he has at times added an interesting statement. He suggests, "Work in your usual relaxed and efficient way." What does he mean by suggesting that I work relaxed and efficient at the same time? I think he knows, as I have learned, that one will work more efficiently if he does not permit himself to get under too much tension and pressure.

I want to close by passing on to you an illustration I discovered some years ago that has meant a great deal to me. Doctor Charles R. Brown was Dean of the Divinity School of Yale University for a number of years. The illustration I want to use comes from one of his books and is the only thing I remember about the book.

Dr. Brown said that there was an old woman who lived outside the city. Her main source of income was from her vegetable garden. She took her vegetables into the city to sell them. One morning she was a little later than usual and had to run with her basket of vegetables on her arm to catch the commuter train. The train was crowded. There was no seat for her. She stood in the aisle with the heavy basket of produce on her arm. Dr. Brown said that after a while a kindly young man touched her on the elbow and said to her, "Pardon me, lady, why don't you put your basket down? The train will carry it and you."

What are you carrying in that basket? Put it down, the Lord will carry it and you.

# SUMMARY

The Christian's life—past, present, and future—is lived in union with Christ. "In Christ" is not only a key to Paul's theological thought, it is *the* key to the Christian life. That life begins when one is brought into union with the resurrected Christ. We are in him and he is in us (chap. 1). Every aspect of our subsequent lives as Christians can be described as "Real Life in Christ." Paul exhorted the Romans and would exhort us to live the transformed life. That transformation takes place as we let the indwelling Christ live in us and express himself through us (chap. 2). It is "in Christ" that meaningful unity can be attained not only between Jew and Gentile but between other human divisions based on culture, color, or conditions of life. In him the dividing walls of hostility are broken down (chap. 3).

Paul challenged the Ephesians and would challenge us to live a life worthy of our calling as Christians (chap. 4) and to live a mature life (chap. 5). Again these goals become increasing realities in our lives as we let Christ live in us and express himself through us. In other words, "the worthy life" and "the mature life" for the Christian are "in him."

If we are to know the fullness of fellowship with him we must deny ourselves, take up our cross, and follow him. If we go all the way with him it will take us by the way of Calvary (chap. 6). We should be grateful, however, that in him the crucifixion is not the end; there follows the empty tomb. Resurrection follows crucifixion just as surely in the life of the child of God as it did in the life of Jesus. Also, both "crucifixion" and "resurrection" refer to or describe a way of life (chap. 7). Finally, if we are to have the peace that passeth understanding we will discover it only through our fellowship with him (chap. 8).

The Christian life begins with our union with Christ, it continues and develops in the consciousness of fellowship with and in him, it ends with the anticipation of life with him in the ages to come. How glorious to be "in Christ" and for him to be in us!

# RESOURCES

BARCLAY, WILLIAM. *The Letters of James and Peter*. "The Daily Bible Study Series." Philadelphia: Westminster Press. (Barclay)

———. *Mind of St. Paul*. New York: Harper & Row, 1959.

*Broadman Bible Commentary, The*. 12 volumes. Nashville: Broadman Press, 1969–1972. (*Broadman*)

*Cambridge Bible for Schools and Colleges, The*. Cambridge University Press. (*Cambridge*)

DEISSMANN, ADOLF. *The Religion of Jesus and the Faith of Paul*. Trans. William E. Wilson. New York: George H. Doran Co., 1926. (Deissmann)

*Expositors' Greek Testament, The*. 5 volumes. New York: George H. Doran Co. (*Expositors'*)

*International Critical Commentary, The*. 38 volumes. Edinburgh: T & T Clark Co. (*International*)

*Interpreter's Bible, The*. 12 volumes. Nashville: Abingdon Press. (*Interpreter's*)

MACKAY, JOHN ALEXANDER. *God's Order*. New York: The Macmillan Co., 1953.

MOFFATT, JAMES. *Moffatt New Testament Commentary, The*. London: Hodder & Stoughton, 1935. (Moffatt)

ROBERTSON, A. T. *Word Pictures in the New Testament*. 6 volumes. Nashville: Broadman Press, 1943. (Robertson)

STEWART, JAMES. *Man in Christ*. New York: Harper & Row, 1935.

*Tyndale New Testament Commentaries*. Wheaton, Ill.: Tyndale House. (*Tyndale*)

VINCENT, MARVIN R. *Word Studies in the New Testament*, 4 volumes. New York: Charles Scribners' Sons, 1957. (Vincent)

GAYLORD

PRINTED IN U.S.A.